National in Gaspésie and Bas-Saint-Laurent

ULYSSES

Parc national de la Gaspésie

1. The highest peak in the Chic-Chocs, Mont Albert, soars 1,154m above sea level.

2. The park's woodland caribou are the last wild herd south of the St. Lawrence River.

3. The wonderful comfort and delicious cuisine at Gîte du Mont-Albert, in the heart of the mountains, make it an excellent value.

4. The Lac aux Américains area is justly considered one of the most beautiful glacial cirques in Québec.

5. Several sites for primitive camping are accessible on foot or by canoe. They offer a unique way to experience the grand natural spaces of Parc national de la Gaspésie.

6. In the winter, several of the park's hiking trails can be used for snowshoeing.

Parc national du Bic

1. A stroll near one of the park's salt marshes may lead to a meeting with a white-tailed deer or water birds.

2. From July to September, Parc national du Bic is the prime location for watching grey seals.

3. For a unique lodging experience in the Île-aux-Amours area, three comfortable yurts are available for rent year-round, and another four are also available in the summer and fall.

4. At the tip of Cap à l'Orignal, hikers enjoy an excellent view of the St. Lawrence.

5. Sea kayakers can enjoy majestic sunsets over the river.

Parc national de l'Île-Bonaventure-et-du-Rocher-Percé

1. The park is home to more than 574 species of vascular plants and more than 200 species of seaweed.

2. The famous Rocher Percé developed millions of years ago from the accumulation of limestone sediment in a warm sea.

3. Île Bonaventure is home to the largest colony of Northern Gannets in the world, with more than 120,000 individuals.

Parc national de Miguasha

1. Park authorities at Parc national de Miguasha have installed a walkway giving easy access to the cliff's fossil riches—a window on the fascinating world of palaeontology.

2. The indispensable guided tour is a trip through time revealing the geological phenomena that formed the park over 380 million years.

3. Miguasha fossils have sparked numerous international scientific studies; the dig teams discover nearly 500 new specimens every year.

Forillon National Park of Canada

1. Nothing compares to sunset sea kayaking near L'Anse-Blanchette.

2. In the Cap-Bon-Ami area, the quiet beaches offer extraordinary views.

3. The cliffs in the North Area of Presqu'île de Forillon plunge spectacularly into the sea.

Table of Contents

List of In-Depth Articles

Research and Writing
France Charest and Olivier Matton
  (parc national de Miguasha)
Alexis de Gheldere (parc national de la Gaspésie)
Alain Demers (parc national du Bic and parc national
de l'Île-Bonaventure-et-du-Rocher-Percé)
Yves Ouellet (Forillon National Park of Canada)

Editor
Claude Morneau

Associate Editor
Pierre Ledoux

Production Director
Olivier Gougeon

Translation
Matthew McLauchlin

Copy Editing
Lynda Hayes

Computer Graphics
Pascal Biet
Marie-France Denis
Isabelle Lalonde
Philippe Thomas

Photography
Front endpaper
Lac Cascapédia, Parc national de la Gaspésie,
© Mathieu Dupuis, Sépaq; Moose, Parc national de la
Gaspésie, © Steve Deschênes, Sépaq
Parc national de la Gaspésie
  1: © Mathieu Dupuis, Sépaq
  2: © Claude Isabel, Sépaq
  3: © Jean-Pierre Huard, Sépaq
  4 to 6: © Sépaq
Parc national du Bic
  1, 4 and 5: © Mathieu Dupuis, Sépaq
  2: © Fred Klus, Sépaq
  3: © Steve Deschênes, Sépaq
Parc national de l'Île-Bonaventure-et-du-Rocher-Percé
  1 and 3: © Jean-Pierre Huard, Sépaq
  2: © Maurice Pitre, Sépaq
Parc national de Miguasha
  1: © Fred Klus, Sépaq
  2: © Jean-Pierre Huard, Sépaq
  3: © Roger Mazerolle, Sépaq
Forillon National Park of Canada
  1 and 2: © Parks Canada / Serge Ouellet
  3: © Parks Canada

Acknowledgements
We wish to thank the staff and administration of the national parks of Québec and Canada for their
collaboration.

The realization of this work was made possible thanks to the financial support of Parcs Québec
and Parks Canada.

Bibliothèque et Archives nationales du Québec and Library and Archives Canada cataloguing in publication

Main entry under title :
          National parks in Gaspésie and Bas-Saint-Laurent
          (Ulysses travel guide)
          Translation of: Les parcs nationaux de la Gaspésie et du Bas-Saint-Laurent.
          Includes index.
          ISBN 978-2-89464-839-1
          1. National parks and reserves - Québec (Province) - Bas-Saint-Laurent-Gaspésie Region - Guidebooks. 2. Bas-
Saint-Laurent-Gaspésie Region (Québec) - Guidebooks. I. Series.
FC2913.P3713 2008   363.6'80971477   C2007-942523-2

© June 2008, Ulysses Travel Guides
All rights reserved
Printed in Canada
ISBN 978-2-89464-839-1

FROM SEA TO SKY

A string of unspoiled protected areas wedged between the sea and the mountains, Québec's national parks in Bas-Saint-Laurent and Gaspésie offer incomparable nature vacations. Amateur hikers, experienced kayakers, Sunday cyclists, camping buffs, nature lovers—all will find something to satisfy their thirst for adventure and new horizons.

This guide will help you plan the perfect trip for your interests and preferences. It will be your reference to the breathtaking landscapes of Bas-Saint-Laurent and Gaspésie, which are destined to be some of your most enduring travel memories.

Ranging along the shore of the St. Lawrence River estuary, the islands, capes and bays of Parc national du Bic will enchant you. The teeming marine life along the shore, including seals and eiders, gives way to forests and grassland as you make your way inland.

At the heart of the Gaspé Peninsula, the stunning, untamed mountains of Parc national de la Gaspésie invite climbers to test their thousand-metre-high peaks. At the foot of the Chic-Chocs mountain range, Gîte du Mont-Albert welcomes hikers with style.

Near Chaleur Bay, Parc national de Miguasha is a treasure trove of marvellously preserved fossils—a priceless record of the distant past that earned the park the title of UNESCO World Heritage Site in 1999.

Rocher Percé may be world-famous, but less well-known is the 5.8km² natural area, Parc national de l'Île-Bonaventure-et-du-Rocher-Percé, that protects it. Île Bonaventure is best known for its large colony of northern gannets, but it shelters dozens of other marine bird species as well.

Grand mountain landscapes, dizzying cliffs plunging into the Gulf of St. Lawrence, pebbled beaches, and rich and varied flora and fauna—all are on display at Forillon National Park of Canada. This 245km² protected area at the eastern tip of the Gaspé peninsula also bears witness to the captivating story of the 20th-century fishers and merchants who lived here.

Protected Areas

Bas-Saint-Laurent and Gaspésie are home to several natural areas protected by the federal and provincial governments. They are available for use for educational and recreational purposes, in keeping with the goal of protecting these natural sites.

Parcs Québec

As part of a vogue for nature conservancy in North America in the late 19th century, the Québec government created the province's first national park, Montagne Tremblante (today Parc national du Mont-Tremblant), in 1895. Since then, the desire to protect the wilderness and make it accessible for recreation has continued to take shape.

With the rise of environmentalism, the 1970s saw a government commitment to create a network of national parks throughout the province. To this end, the *Parks Act* was passed in 1997, and a Parks Policy was introduced in 1982. These initiatives led to the creation of the Parcs Québec network, which was placed under the responsibility of Société des établissements de plein air du Québec (Sépaq) in 1999.

The Parcs Québec network is based on the division of Québec into 43 natural regions and the identification of exceptional natural heritage sites in the province. The parks network's mission is "to ensure the conservation and permanent protection of areas representative of the natural regions of Québec and of natural sites with outstanding features, in particular because of their biological diversity, while providing the public with access to those areas or sites for educational or cross-country recreation purposes."

Accordingly, the Québec national park network meets the criteria of the International Union for Conservation of Nature (IUCN). The goal of each of Québec's national parks is to ensure the conservation of its land, in particular through an Ecological Integrity Monitoring Program, and to offer a variety of interpretive and recreational programs allowing visitors to discover the full importance, richness, and individual character of each park. Parcs Québec continually ensures that park installations (discovery and visitors centre, trails, campgrounds, etc.) respect sensitive areas and impact nature as little as possible.

This travel guide to the nature parks of Gaspésie and Bas-Saint-Laurent offers you numerous ways to experience the parks and have a memorable vacation.

Parks Canada

Canada's network of national parks is one of the oldest in the world. Since 1885, Canada has created 42 national parks and national park reserves, protecting ecosystems representing Canada's major natural regions.

Forillon National Park of Canada was the first federal national park in Québec. Since its creation in 1970, it has protected a representative landscape of the Notre-Dame and Mégantic mountain regions and the Gulf of St. Lawrence marine region. It is recognized as a key nature preserve, protecting unique natural environments, diverse habitats, and endangered species. It also bears witness to its past human inhabitants, with numerous culturally and historically significant vestiges offering evidence of human adaptation to the natural world.

Forillon National Park offers visitors a panoply of recreational and interpretative activities on the water, on the shore, and inland, giving visitors the chance to discover, learn, and grow.

Parks Canada's mandate ties together the protection, discovery, and appreciation of Canada's natural heritage. Protecting the ecological integrity and cultural resources of Forillon National Park ensures that visitors can enjoy a unique opportunity to connect with the sea, the mountains, and the recent and distant heritage of local communities, now and for years to come.

This connection with the natural and cultural landscape both familiarizes visitors with Parks Canada's mandate and inspires them to act to protect our ecological and human heritage. The visitors' experience is thus at the heart of the agency's responsibilities, along with education and the protection of ecological and cultural resources.

Responsible Behaviour

Each year, thousands of people visit Québec's national parks. This intense usage can have an impact on the natural environment. Responsible behaviour helps preserve the parks. It is therefore very important to be familiar with park rules. It is also useful to follow the recommendations of *Leave No Trace Canada*, the Canadian version of the popular American *Leave No Trace* program. This program aims to raise awareness of the impact of recreational activities and ways of preventing or mitigating this impact. Rather than a set of rules, *Leave No Trace Canada* is instead an educative and ethical program. Below is a summary.

Leave No Trace Principles

■ Plan Ahead and Prepare

• Know the regulations and special concerns for the area you'll visit.

• Prepare for extreme weather, hazards, and emergencies.

• Schedule your trip to avoid times of high use.

• Visit in small groups. Split larger parties into groups of four to six people.

• Repackage food to minimize waste.

• Use a map and compass to eliminate the use of marking paint, rock cairns or flagging.

■ Travel and Camp on Durable Surfaces

• Durable surfaces include established trails and campsites, rock, gravel, dry grasses or snow.

• Protect riparian areas by camping at least 70 metres from lakes and streams.

• Good campsites are found, not made. Altering a site is not necessary.

• In popular areas:

> • Concentrate use on existing trails and campsites.
> • Walk single file in the middle of the trail, even when wet or muddy.
> • Keep campsites small. Focus activity in areas where vegetation is absent.

• In pristine areas:

> • Disperse use to prevent the creation of campsites or trails.
> • Avoid places where impacts are just beginning.

■ Dispose of Waste Properly

• Pack it in, pack it out. Inspect your campsite and rest areas for trash or spilled foods. Pack out all trash, leftover food, and litter.

- Deposit solid human waste in catholes dug 15 to 20 centimetres deep at least 70 metres from water, camp, and trails. Cover and disguise the cathole when finished.

- Pack out toilet paper and hygiene products.

- To wash yourself or your dishes, carry water 70 metres away from streams or lakes and use small amounts of biodegradable soap. Scatter strained dishwater.

■ Leave What You Find

- Preserve the past: examine, but do not touch, cultural or historic structures and artifacts.

- Leave rocks, plants and other natural objects as you find them.

- Do not pick or transport plants.

- Do not build structures or furniture or dig trenches.

■ Minimize the Impact of Campfires

- Campfires can cause lasting impacts to the backcountry. Use a lightweight stove for cooking and enjoy a candle lantern for light.

- Where fires are permitted, use established fire rings, fire pans, or mound fires.

- Keep fires small.

- Burn all wood and coals to ash, put out campfires completely, and then scatter the cool ashes.

Pets

In Québec's parks, such as Bic, Miguasha, Gaspésie, and Île-Bonaventure-et-du-Rocher-Percé, the only domesticated animals allowed are service dogs helping disabled persons, or dogs in training to become service dogs.

In federal parks, such as Forillon National Park, pets are allowed in certain areas as long as they are kept on a leash at all times.

■ Respect Wildlife

- Observe wildlife from a distance. Do not follow or approach them.

- Never feed animals. Feeding wildlife damages their health, alters natural behaviours, and exposes them to predators and other dangers.

- Protect wildlife and your food by storing rations and trash securely.

- Control pets at all times, or leave them at home.

From Sea to Sky - Responsible Behaviour

- Avoid wildlife during sensitive times such as when they are mating, nesting, raising young or in the winter.

■ Be Considerate of Other Visitors

- Respect other visitors and protect the quality of their experience.

- Be courteous. Yield to other users on the trail.

- Step to the downhill side of the trail when encountering horseback riders.

- Take breaks and camp away from trails and other visitors.

- Let nature's sounds prevail. Avoid loud voices and noises.

Wildlife Watching

Certain animal species are rare, while others are restricted to a specific environment. To increase your chances of seeing some, opt for sites where they're certain to be—for example, in July, visitors to Parc national de l'Île-Bonaventure-et-du-Rocher-Percé are sure to see a multitude of seabirds, especially the northern gannet colony.

In Parc national de la Gaspésie, hikers have a good chance, though not a guarantee, of spotting caribou at the summits of Mont Albert and Mont Jacques-Cartier. The herd includes fewer than 200 head of caribou distributed over a wide territory. An exhibition on this majestic animal can be seen at the foot of Mont Jacques-Cartier and along the trail to the mountaintop.

However, it takes more than abundance to give visitors the chance to observe a species. Visitors must also be constantly on the lookout. Being discreet and being curious are the keys to success. Walking slowly along the trails and looking off in the distance along the shores also help.

Binoculars are a good way to make a nature safari more interesting, but it is best to look around with the naked eye first. A good field guide to birds is also most useful. Besides bookstores, bird guides are also sold at the national parks' Boutique Nature shops. Visitors can also consult the websites of Sépaq *(www.sepaq.com)* and Parks Canada *(www.pc.gc.ca)* for information on the bird species in each park.

Preparing for a Hike

Here are some tips for making the best of your hiking experience:

Get Your Bearings

Each year, hikers get lost in the forest because they wander and lose track of landmarks. Fortunately, it's easy to find your way in national parks thanks to their well-marked network of prepared trails.

As signs are simply indications, it's better to rely on a map of the trails, usually available at the Information Kiosk. Maps allow you to find a trail that suits you, and to tell where you are at any time, just like on the highway. Don't start hiking without one!

If you are a new hiker or if you are hiking with children, choose short trails that aren't too steep. It won't take long to return to the beginning of the trail, and you can decide then whether or not to try another trail.

Know the Conditions

Check the weather forecast for the day on the Environment Canada Web site. Even if the weather in town is fine, the weather may be different in the park, especially if it is at a high altitude.

Choose the Right Shoes

Large leather walking boots are not appropriate for one- to two-hour hikes. It's better to choose comfortable sports shoes that support the foot well.

However, if you intend to regularly spend a good part of the day walking, taking sloping paths to reach beautiful views, light walking boots are more appropriate. These shoes, often made of thin leather and Cordura, are reinforced at the ankle for better lateral support, resulting in less fatigue and fewer risks of sprains.

As hiking becomes more and more popular, light walking boots are now being sold even in regular shoe stores. But be careful! Such boots are usually uncomfortable, with an insole that is flat rather than contoured to your foot, and a poor quality outer sole that can split. Stick to specialized camping stores.

Bring Water

Water is crucial fuel for hikers; never go hiking without it. As you expend energy and get hot, you will dehydrate rapidly. If you allow yourself to become thirsty, you will become impatient to return, ruining the pleasure of the hike.

For a short hike, one 500ml bottle will suffice; for hikes of two hours or longer, bring at least two. Certain waist packs can carry two bottles without being heavy or cumbersome.

Water in the wilderness is not safe to drink, no matter how clean it looks. Never drink it. It may contain parasites from animal excrement, which cause diseases such as giardiasis, whose symptoms (diarrhea and weakness) are similar to "Montezuma's revenge."

On long hikes, it may be impossible to carry all the water you'll need. In such cases, you can refill from a spring or small creek, provided you take steps to make the water potable.

Camping supply stores sell filters that can remove the *Giardia* parasite (responsible for giardiasis) from water. According to their manufacturers, these filters have pores 2 microns in size, while the *Giardia* parasite in water is 8 to 15 microns in diameter.

Another method is to purify the water with 2% tincture of iodine, sold in pharmacies. Add two to four drops for each litre of water, mix well, and wait 30 minutes before drinking to ensure that the parasites are killed.

Boiling water is also a good way to prevent disease. After boiling, let the water sit for a few minutes, then stir well to oxygenate it and get rid of any off taste.

Dress Appropriately

Even if you feel like going out in jeans or shorts and a T-shirt, bring other clothes in your bag to protect yourself from insects or to keep warm when you stop. Avoid cotton clothes, and dress in layers.

Light colours attract fewer insects. Choose loose shirts and pants that close well at the end of their sleeves and legs. Wear a cap to protect yourself from insect bites and stings, the sun, and the rain.

Don't forget a sweater, windbreaker, or light rain jacket. The temperature can change while you are hiking, and when you stop to admire the view, the wind can chill you quickly.

Prepare Your Backpack

Even for a quick walk on a trail, you should never leave without a backpack. Pack a bottle of water, of course, some fruits and nuts, and some good-sized sandwiches if you'll be out long.

To avoid blackflies and other bugs, bring insect repellent. Citronella works well, as long as you reapply it frequently and cover your skin thoroughly. Citronella is also less toxic than the traditional DEET (diethyltoluamide).

Don't forget to add a compact survival kit with a first aid kit and an emergency blanket. You can buy these kits in camping supply stores. A Swiss Army knife is also useful, as well as a lighter for lighting a fire in an emergency.

Walking Poles

Walking poles are increasingly popular. Sold in sporting goods stores, they can be very helpful on long-distance or sloped trails. They help maintain balance and offer support when needed, reduce leg effort, and ease pressure on the knees when going downhill.

Protect Yourself from Mosquitoes

Proper clothing and insect repellent are not all you can do to protect yourself from mosquitoes. You should also avoid scented products, even slightly scented ones, because they attract insects. Pack neutral, unscented soap, and use shampoo, deodorant, and antiperspirant that are as neutral as possible.

If you are bitten, apply calamine lotion to the bite. Itching can be eased with a paste made of water and baking soda.

These precautions are important since the discomfort of insect bites and stings can make your expedition much less pleasant.

The Well-Equipped Camper

Visitors looking forward to a longer stay in one of Québec's national parks can stay in one of the inns, cabins, yurts, or shelters at their disposal. But those who want an even more authentic outdoor experience can camp in a tent (reservations strongly recommended). If there is no room or if the park doesn't allow camping, you can always use a private campground near the park.

Parc national du Bic and Parc national de la Gaspésie offer a limited number of campsites under a turnkey package, including a camping trailer or Huttopia tent, cooking equipment, electricity, heating, potable running water, and access to washroom facilities. However, the majority of campsites have much more rustic facilities, though some do offer certain services. It is therefore important to bring the right equipment. Besides the tent and sleeping bag, a number of accessories can help make camping more comfortable:

- A tarpaulin. Bring a big nylon tarpaulin to increase your living space; with a bit of rope and some stakes, it will prove very helpful when putting up the tent or cooking.

- A ground mattress. Anybody who has ever inflated a mattress will appreciate a self-inflating one. Roll it up and it stows compactly; unroll it and it inflates automatically. No more pumping! An open-cell foam inside the mattress improves the comfort value.

- A battery-powered fluorescent lantern. In a small tent, an ultra-compact candle lantern provides sufficient illumination and reduces damp.

- A propane stove. A two-burner model is the most practical for a family. It takes up more room than a small camp stove, but is much more stable. However, if space and weight are issues, a camp stove is more practical. Some models are so compact that they fit in a lunch box.

- A cooking set. These have changed greatly in recent years. No longer for just one person, some include a set of three pots with lids that double as frying pans thanks to removable handles. Teflon-coated cookware is available.

- Dishes and utensils. Many specialty stores sell unbreakable Lexan dishes (high-density plastic) and utensils. Individual place settings in net bags, including a bowl, plate, cup, and utensils, are available.

- Cooler. A cooler is indispensable for food and drink. A 70-litre size is perfect for a family of four. To avoid messes caused by melting ice, store food in plastic containers.

Start by Renting

Many camping supply stores rent basic camping equipment, a good option if you are not yet sure you will enjoy camping out.

Basic equipment can include a six- to eight-person tent (perfect for a family of four with gear), three-season sleeping bags, self-inflating mattresses, and a two-burner propane stove.

Each article can be rented separately. A deposit is usually required. When you return, the store may offer to deduct part or all of the rental fee from the purchase of similar equipment.

Reserving a Campsite

National parks offer wonderful holidays in beautiful natural settings. Several types of sites are available, including semi-serviced, primitive, and group campgrounds.

■ Parcs Québec

In Québec's national parks, camping reservations open on January 15; for other accommodations (cabins, inns, yurts, etc.), reservations can be made year-round.

For a better choice of sites when you want them, you can reserve up to four months in advance. In the high season, there are often sites available but you may not be able to get the site you prefer. You can reserve over the Internet or by telephone, paying the full fee by credit card.

From Sea to Sky - The Well-Equipped Camper

■ Parks Canada

Reservations for Forillon National Park are accepted starting in April, by phone and on the Internet.

A quarter of the 367 semi-serviced campsites are kept available for campers who do not make reservations, on a first-come, first-served basis.

Information and Reservations

Parcs Québec
☎ 1-800-665-6527
www.sepaq.com

Parks Canada
☎ 1-877-737-3783 or 514-335-4813 (from outside North America)
www.pccamping.ca

PARC NATIONAL DU BIC

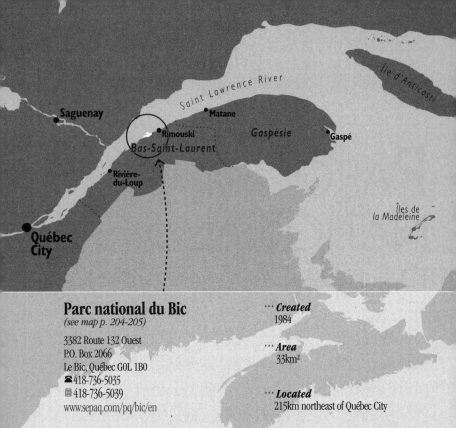

Parc national du Bic
(see map p. 204-205)

3382 Route 132 Ouest
P.O. Box 2066
Le Bic, Québec G0L 1B0
☎ 418-736-5035
🖩 418-736-5039
www.sepaq.com/pq/bic/en

··· *Created*
1984

··· *Area*
33km²

··· *Located*
215km northeast of Québec City

Our Highlights

- The interpretive trail revealing the park's historic, archaeological, and natural heritage.

- The Pic-Champlain lookout, with an unbeatable view of the whole island, including the estuary and the islands.

- Wildlife watching: depending on the season, visitors can see white-tailed deer, seals, and eiders.

- The magnificent sunsets.

Visiting Time

···*One hour*

If you are just passing through Parc national du Bic, stop at the Discovery and Visitors Centre to see the exhibition *A Legacy of the Sea*, which offers an overview of the park's attractions and will probably make you want to stay longer or visit again.

···*A half-day*

With a half-day, you can enjoy the minibus excursion to the park's main attractions: Île aux Amours, Cap Caribou, Pointe aux Épinettes, the Rioux farm, and the spectacular Pic-Champlain lookout.

···*A day or more*

If you are staying for a day or more in the park, you can explore it independently. Depending on the season, you can explore the hiking, cycling, snowshoeing, or skiing trails along the magnificent shoreline, or take a sea kayak trip or a cruise to meet the seals and seabirds.

Mountains plunging into the river, scores of seabirds flocking to bays and nesting on headlands and islands, seals basking on the riverbank—Parc national du Bic is all these and more. Its name comes from the French word "bec" or its variant "biec," meaning point or peak, and indeed its points and peaks are front-row seats for some of the most extraordinary and beautiful sunsets in the world. However, this park is still little known among many nature lovers from Québec and abroad.

Some History

The First Residents

The last ice age 13,000 years ago left the area as barren sea, ice, desert, rock, and gravel. It took 3,000 years for vegetation to reestablish itself—simple tundra-like plants at first, then coniferous forest 8,500 years ago.

Accordingly, the first signs of human habitation date back between 8,000 and 9,000 years. Small groups of Aboriginal people from the south came to explore the land "recently" freed by the retreat of the glaciers. At the time, the water levels were 155m higher than they are now. The new arrivals settled temporarily on the shore of a fjord in what is now the Rivière Sud-Ouest valley, an area resembling today's estuary.

These nomadic hunters and fishers were the descendants of the first inhabitants of the continent, who had arrived from Asia 12,000 years ago via the then-dry Bering Strait.

They hunted caribou and perhaps also big game of the Pleistocene age. They probably also enjoyed the molluscs, fish, and sea mammals of the cold Arctic waters.

During the Archaic period (8,000 to 2,500 years ago), the occupants took a wider variety of game and fish, but did not yet know how to farm or make pottery.

Over the last 2,000 years of archaeological time, traces of human habitation become more and more abundant, probably because of an increased population. The great variety of artifacts found during archaeological digs at Le Bic suggest that the region was temporarily inhabited by nomadic groups trading with peoples living far away.

During the period of European contact, the region was frequented by small groups of Innu from north of the gulf. The region appears to have been a stopping point for everyone travelling on the river.

Pic Champlain was a very useful landmark, and Havre du Bic and Îles Bic and Bicquette were an important stop for river travellers. Furthermore, the Rivière du Sud-Ouest valley and adjoining valleys offered an access route inland.

From the Seigneurial Period to Present Times

Aboriginal people, explorers, and missionaries at first passed through this territory without settling. Seigneuries were set up, Le Bic in 1675 and Baie du Ha! Ha! in 1751, and the territory began to be used for seasonal activities such as fishing and fur trading.

The first settlers arrived in 1822 with the first resident seigneur, Archibald Campbell, settling on the St. Lawrence River bank and cultivating the land.

With the abolition of the seigneurial system in 1855, the parishes of Le Bic and Saint-Fabien became municipalities. During the second half of the 19th century, the region's economy was mostly based on forestry.

Agriculture was becoming much more important around the turn of the 20th century. The current national park preserves a house and farm that belonged to the Rioux family for several generations.

The presence of the river constantly influenced the land now protected by the park. Pic Champlain was a major landmark for navigators, and innumerable mariners moored in Havre du Bic, a gathering point for more than a century.

Local people came in great numbers to stroll or gather soft-shell clams. Botanists were drawn to the area to observe and catalogue its flora, unique to this place where river and mountains meet; numerous species of rare and arctic-alpine plants are found here.

A summer camp in the Cap-à-l'Orignal area helped make the splendour of the site known to more people. The enchanting site became a very popular vacation spot for rich Americans and English-Canadians.

Finally, in 1984, the government of Québec created Parc national du Bic to protect an area representative of the natural region of the south shore of the St. Lawrence estuary. This new status put an end to certain activities incompatible with a protected area, such as logging and private cottaging. However, gathering softshell clams continues in some areas as part of local tradition.

Geography and Geology

The Appalachians and the Estuary

The site of a spectacular meeting between the Appalachians and the St. Lawrence estuary, Parc national du Bic extends between the municipalities of Saint-Fabien-sur-Mer and Le Bic, north of Route 132. A little more than half of the park's area (18.8km²) is dry land, while the other half (14.4km²) is underwater either all the time or at high tide.

The strongly indented 30km shoreline hides many secrets in its narrow bays and coves, from Anse à Capelans in the west to Havre du Bic in the east. The sharp relief is striking, with its rocky ridges parallel to the river. The park's several peaks are part of the Appalachian chain, a mountain range extending 3,000km from Alabama to Newfoundland.

Tiny islands dot the river near the shore; the largest, Île aux Amours, measures scarcely 0.1km².

Geology

Two hundred million years of erosion has left the Appalachians with rounded tops instead of the sharp peaks they once had. The glaciations and high sea levels of the Quaternary period also left their mark.

The relief in Le Bic is largely the product of tectonic movement, the passage of glaciers, and the presence of ancient seas. The rough terrain consists of ancient rock formations sculpted by erosion.

Though softened by erosion, the coastal range has stayed steep, with ridges, thrust and strike-slip faults, and sea terraces. This new millennium will see the cold salt water continue to change the landscape little by little. Waves, for example, stir up sediments, mixing and redistributing them as beaches, spits, and the like.

All these phenomena and many more are explained in detail at the park's Discovery and Visitors Centre and in its discovery activities.

Features of the Park

The Natural Landscape

The national park overlooks the St. Lawrence River estuary, a transitional zone between the river and the sea. Tides range from 3m to 5m. The river here looks as vast as the sea since the estuary is 30km to 50km wide.

The depth of the estuary varies between 300m and 350m. The water is especially cold, less than 4.5°C, though the park's bays and coves have water temperatures between 10°C and 15°C.

The climate is strongly influenced by the estuary, which plays a stabilizing role, reducing temperature extremes. This produces milder winters and cooler summers than inland.

Autumn and spring both come late. The warmest month, July, reaches an average temperature of 17°C, while the coldest, January, is –12°C on average.

The shore and marine zone are not the park's only natural areas near the river. It also hosts a forest, fields, and peat bogs.

■ Forest

The most remarkable characteristic of this forest is its remarkable transition from the familiar deciduous forest of more densely populated areas to the typically nordic coniferous forest.

The Pic-Champlain trail passes through a small maple grove that was once used as a sugar bush. The forest that covers the summit of Pic Champlain largely consists of conifers such as balsam fir and white spruce.

In Parc national du Bic, no fewer than seven exceptional forest ecosystems (EFEs) have been listed by the Ministère des Ressources naturelles et de la Faune. Among these is a white spruce stand with lichens, extending along the bar south of Cap Enragé, a wide band linking the cape to the mainland. A fir forest with cedars and white spruce covers part of Pic Champlain, while a stand of jack pine south of Baie du Ha! Ha! is another jewel of the area.

■ Fields

Parc national du Bic encompasses a few fields, some left fallow and others still cultivated. Nowadays, only grains and hay are grown.

The fallow fields are experiencing a gradual regeneration of the forest. The oldest abandoned field, on the bar between Cap Caribou and Cap Enragé, is an excellent example, with a new stand of white spruce and a wide variety of plants.

■ Peat Bogs

After the retreat of the prehistoric Goldthwait Sea 12,500 years ago, pools of water formed along the shores and gradually filled with vegetation. The abundance of sphagnum moss caused the water to become acidic, preventing decomposition and allowing organic matter to accumulate—thereby forming peat bogs.

Unlike marshes, peat bogs fill in from the surface down. This strange environment is host to many unusual plants, including carnivores such as the famous pitcher plant, which draws insects in with its perfumed leaves and traps them on its sticky surface.

■ Shore

The shore takes numerous forms, forming capes, cliffs, and bays. The windswept shores are home to resilient conifers such as white spruce, balsam fir, and white cedar.

There are a few deciduous trees, mainly small stands of white birch, alders, and junipers. Lichens and mosses grow on rocks, as in the tundra.

■ Salt Marshes

The coastline is also home to three salt marshes: one near Pointe aux Épinettes, one opposite Île aux Amours, and a third at the mouth of Rivière du Sud-Ouest. The shores are muddy because they are lapped by the tides, and the vegetation mainly consists of spartina with rushes and sedge grass in the areas that are flooded less often.

The marshes are fringed by bushes such as alders and willows. Several species of waterbirds live, feed, or nest here, such as Sandpipers, Black Ducks, and Great Blue Herons.

Flora

The great diversity of habitats has produced an astonishing variety of plants. The park is home to no fewer than 700 species of vascular plants, nearly a third of all vascular plant species in Québec—an enormous figure for such a small area. The following section describes just a few of the plants that grow in the park; to find out more, ask at the Discovery and Visitors Centre about the many nature discovery activites organized by the park.

■ Arctic-Alpine Plants

These plants mostly grow north of the tree line but can be found more rarely in southern habitats that are open and cold enough. The coast of Parc national du Bic offers such an environment, especially on its windswept, eroded cliffs and escarpments. Trees cannot grow here because of the limestone bedrock, thin soil, and exposure to cold and salty air.

■ Rare Plants

Parc national du Bic is famous for its wealth of rare species, due in large part to the sand, rock and limestone coastline, as well as the maritime climate. Many species cannot grow here, while many of those that do, grow in few other places.

The Park's Wild Rosebushes

Parc national du Bic is renowned for its marvellous and extremely diverse flora, including the superb native roses. Of Québec's wild rose species, two (*Rosa williamsii* and *Rosa rousseauiorum*) are found only in the province. In particular, *Rosa williamsii* is found only in Bas-Saint-Laurent, with the largest population in Parc national du Bic.

Be sure to look for them during your visit, and enjoy the chance to view and smell one of the most beautiful wildflowers in the world, with lovely colours and a unique, enchanting perfume.

Parc national du Bic — Features of the Park - Flora

Of just over 400 rare plant taxa in Québec, Parc national du Bic harbours over 20. No fewer than 17 of these species are on Québec's list of vascular plants at risk of being classified as threatened or vulnerable—a good reason to obey park regulations and stay on the paths.

Some of these fragile plants, such as the ones on the cornice of Pic Champlain, have been damaged in the past by overly adventuresome hikers. Since 2001, the plants have been protected by nets and information panels.

■ Invasive Non-Indigenous Plants

Of the hundreds of vascular plant species in the park, about 25% are exotic in origin. The most worrisome invasive species is certainly the smooth bedstraw (*Galium mollugo*). This prolific plant threatens the ecological diversity even in the meadows.

Another exotic plant, wild chervil (*Anthriscus sylvestris*), has spread widely along footpaths.

Finally, purple loosestrife (*Lythrum salicaria*) has become established in the freshwater marsh along the eastern side of the Baie des Cochons saltwater marsh. It can also be found on the southern edge of the Havre du Bic marsh.

A native of Eurasia, purple loosestrife has spread widely throughout North America, colonizing marshes and roadside culverts. Unfortunately, it is gradually replacing other plants. In Parc national du Bic, however, its expansion is limited by the salt water nearby.

■ Wetland Vegetation

Salt marshes: This rich and productive habitat's appearance depends on how often it is submerged by the tides. The more rarely flooded areas farther from the shore are host to abundant Baltic rushes, sedges, and maritime bulrushes.

Areas that are only rarely lapped by the tides are ideal for alternate-flowered spartina, while muddy and sandy foreshores are host to rockweed, which clings to gravel and rocks.

Peat bogs: Labrador tea, bog bedstraw, and low birch are among the most common bog species. Bogs are also home to carnivorous plants such as the pitcher plant, which grows in no other habitat.

Beside lakes and rivers: In 2005 alone, 56 species of vascular plants were identified in the park for the first time. The areas richest in newly found plants were bodies of fresh water, such as the shores of Lac à Crapauds, the marshes south of Mont Chocolat and near the Baie des Cochons salt marshes, the ponds in the campground, and the banks of Rivière du Sud-Ouest.

The river is primarily lined with deciduous trees such as willows and alders. The underbrush is home to ferns, such as the fiddlehead or ostrich fern, which resembles a large feather. Near the waterfall, an old farm is home to black and red ash trees, a rare sight in the area.

The seaside: The park's coastline is home to some 70 seaside plant species, including seaweed and other algae—some 20 species of green algae, as many species of red algae, and some 30 species of brown algae.

Their colour depends on the amount of light they receive in their preferred habitat. Red algae, such as Irish moss, rarely spread above the low tide mark. The foreshore between the lowest tide mark and median high tide mark is the preferred haunt of rockweed, wrack, and bladder-wrack. These brown algae species shelter and feed a profusion of marine invertebrates such as gammarids, whelks, and periwinkles.

Numerous masses of cast-up seaweed can be seen on beaches and rocks; these include blade kelp, dulse, and sea colander.

Rocky or sandy areas between the high-tide line and the coastal forest are home to halophytes, or plants that live in brackish water. These include various species of atriplexes and certain herbaceous plants. One interesting halophyte is the seaside ragwort, a beautiful colony of which can be seen at the top of the beach at Baie du Ha! Ha!.

At the forest edge, large colonies of sand ryegrass grow together with wild roses. The rocky ground is home to blue flag irises, red currants, and serviceberries.

Wildlife Watching

The variety of habitats in Parc national du Bic brings with it a corresponding diversity of animal species. From woods to marshes, from mountains to shoreline, the national park is a particularly rich area for wildlife.

The presence of numerous animal species in Parc national du Bic does not guarantee that you will see them; but with some species, your chances are excellent.

Fish

The estuary is home to some 50 fish species. The banks are a spawning ground for herring and capelin, which form an important food source for seals and whales.

■ Capelin

From May to July, visitors can enjoy an extraordinary spectacle: capelin in the thousands casting themselves up on the beach to lay and fertilize millions of eggs. The endless beached capelin are a godsend for shorebirds and seabirds, such as Gulls and terns.

■ Tomcod

Tomcod spend the summer here after climbing rivers in the thousands in December and January, most notably Rivière Sainte-Anne between Trois-Rivières and Québec City. In Sainte-Anne-de-la-Pérade, icefishers wait for them in huts set up on the ice.

■ Salmon

Rivière du Sud-Ouest is home to a population of about forty salmon. Their small population is explained in part by the presence of a small waterfall, which blocks off all but a tiny part of the river. Because of their precarious situation, fishing them was banned even before the park was created, and of course remains so today.

■ American Eel

Until quite recently, the eel fishery was an important autumn activity in the region. Local people caught these fish using a method the first Europeans learned from Aboriginal people, using weirs erected perpendicular to the bank to lead the eels into traps.

In 1997, about a hundred weirs were set up in the Gulf of St. Lawrence, but the fishery was closed in 2004 due to an alarming decline in stocks over the previous 20 years.

A study carried out in Rivière du Sud-Ouest has increased scientific knowledge of the eel's life cycle. These fish live in the river for 6 to 20 years before setting out for the

Sargasso Sea in the Atlantic, 1,500km from the Florida coast between Bermuda and the Bahamas. The eels reproduce there between February and April before dying.

Following a slow seven-year journey, the young, called elvers, return to the mouth of Rivière du Sud-Ouest in late June and early July. Many of the elvers remain in brackish or salt water.

Park wardens present talks about these mysterious travellers at the Discovery and Visitors Centre.

Small Sea Creatures

■ Softshell Clam

The softshell clam, colloquially called *clam* even in French, is probably the best known mollusc in Parc national du Bic. It is a food source for numerous animals, such as Cormorants, Kittiwakes, and Gulls, as well as fish such as winter flounder, halibut, and cod.

The softshell clam is widely harvested, a custom whose extent, quantity, period, and location are tightly regulated by the federal government. These restrictions must be taken seriously, especially since they deal with the possibility of toxic contamination. Some of the algae that the clams feed on can contain a paralysing toxin or domoic acid, which can cause nervous system disorders and even death; other biotoxins produced by algae in the St. Lawrence, though not fatal, can cause severe digestive and intestinal disorders.

■ Blue Mussel

Widespread on the Le Bic shore, blue mussels are easy to find on the foreshore at low tide. They are almost always fixed to rocks or gravel by a web of tiny filaments known as byssus. This filter feeder, distinguished by its blue-black shell, is the main food source for the Common Eider.

■ Macoma Clam

The macoma clam, which lives at the edge of the beach, is the third most common bivalve (two-shelled mollusc) on the Le Bic coast. Similar to the softshell clam, this mollusc is scarcely more than 1.5cm in diameter.

The macoma clam digs into the beach; in some spots, an average of 1,300 individuals can be found in one cubic metre of sand.

■ Periwinkles

These creatures are found gripping the submerged surfaces of rocks, amid seaweed. These little cone-shaped molluscs can survive out of the water if they are kept out of the sun, and also withstand variations in salinity.

■ Urchins

Dense populations of green sea urchins can be found north of Cap à l'Orignal and around Récif à l'Orignal. These little creatures are a major part of the Common Eider's diet.

It is even possible that their abundance influences the winter distribution of groups of eiders along the coast. Before ice forms, these sea ducks have a marked preference for shallow areas near reefs, where they easily find urchins and mussels.

Mammals

Parc national du Bic is home to at least fifteen land and sea mammal species. The following are the most interesting.

■ Porcupine

Besides the beaver, the American porcupine is the area's largest rodent. In the early 1990s, the porcupine population on Montagne à Michaud and Cap à l'Orignal reached 40 individuals/km², one of the highest densities in North America.

Scientists explain that Le Bic offers excellent porcupine habitats. The topography offers numerous rocky mounds and scree slopes that porcupines can use as dens, especially in the cold season. Near these shelters are many conifers such as white pine and balsam fir, whose bark is an important food source in winter.

Finally, the fisher, a mammal similar to a weasel and the porcupine's natural predator, used to be relatively rare in the area. Nowadays, however, the fisher is becoming more common, and porcupines have left many areas where they once abounded. However, this is only temporary, as the porcupines and fishers live in a cyclic pattern of abundance.

■ White-Tailed Deer

Although moose are rare in the park, white-tailed deer are a familiar sight, feeding in the numerous regenerating woods.

In less than a decade, the population has shot up from just a few individuals to more than a hundred. Today's milder winters kill fewer individuals from exhaustion and famine resulting from thick snow hampering their movements.

Contrary to popular belief, these animals do not hide away in dense forests, but freely move through open spaces, especially in the evening, making them easier to spot.

Among other areas, white-tailed deer frequent the Pointe aux Épinettes salt marsh, the fields, and the edges of the Rivière-du-Sud-Ouest and Rioux campgrounds.

■ Seals

It is not surprising that seals arouse the most interest of the park's sea mammals. The harbour seal lives year-round in the estuary, while the grey seal arrives as a seasonal visitor. Both species frequent the Cap à l'Orignal area as well as the reefs of Anse à l'Orignal and Anse des Pilotes.

While exploring the park, you will probably see the harbour seal, symbol of Parc national du Bic. This little seal, easy to spot from the shore, is only half the size of the grey seal, which arrives in mid-July.

The Seals of Parc National du Bic

One of the best places in Québec for seal watching, Parc national du Bic is home to two species: the grey seal (*Halichoerus grypus*) and the park's symbol, the harbour seal (*Phoca vitulina*). Easy to spot from the shore, this playful little seal lives in the St. Lawrence estuary year-round. The grey seal, for its part, arrives in the waters of the park in late July. Depending on the height of the tide, both species can be spotted on their haulout grounds, boulders in the park's bays and coves where they gather to rest, mate, or moult. These grounds are located mainly in the Pointe-aux-Épinettes and L'Anse-aux-Bouleaux-Ouest areas; visitors must stay within the seal-watching area.

Harbour seals are distinguished by their little round heads and slightly flattened noses. On the haulout grounds, they assume a characteristic "banana position," with head held up and hind limbs lifted and clenched together.

When high tide submerges their boulders, seals find themselves swimming. They then become difficult to see; visitors must look for their heads emerging from the surface. However, if you are not too far away, this is not difficult.

The ease with which visitors spot harbour seals may lead them to believe that they are abundant everywhere. However, although Parc national du Bic and nearby reefs are home to about 150 harbour seals and 50 grey seals in summer, the estuary population is considered fragile. As a year-round resident of the estuary, the harbour seal is subject to the same pressures as the beluga.

This is something to consider when watching seals. If you get too close, you will scare the seal and drive it off its rock. However, seals' time out of the water is crucial for nursing, moulting, or simply resting. Seals need to be left alone to bask peacefully in the sun.

Above all, never attempt to help a beached seal pup, even if it seems to be in distress. Still inexperienced and unaware of danger, it has simply not paid attention to the receding tide. Picking it up to carry it back to the water will do nothing but mark it with human scent. This will probably lead to it being abandoned by its mother, who at any rate is probably nearby.

Harbour seal: The harbour seal spends a great deal of time sunning itself on uncovered boulders and reefs, which are peaceful but offer a quick escape back to the water in case of danger. When the tide returns, seals leave their haulout (resting and gathering area for the moult) and feed on fish, such as herring and plaice.

In summer, the females (cows) can be seen with their pups. They give birth in May and June on rocky outcroppings protected from the waves. Most births are single, but cases of twins have been reported.

Grey seal: The area's grey seals are part of the Northwest Atlantic population, which breeds mainly on the ice of the Northumberland Strait (between Prince Edward Island and New Brunswick) and on Sable Island (off Nova Scotia). This population has been growing since the 1960s, but the size of the estuary herd is unknown. Parc national du Bic hosts about 50 grey seals.

Though some are occasionally spotted in April, most arrive before the moulting period in May and June, drawn by the abundance of fish. They remain until November, leaving the estuary to breed after the feeding season.

Grey seals spend relatively little time on haulout sites, and avoid sandy beaches and areas accessible from the mainland. In the Gulf of St. Lawrence and the estuary, grey seals feed on some 20 species of fish, mainky capelin and cod, and a few invertebrates.

Birds

At least 200 species of birds have been spotted in Parc national du Bic. The coastal waters of the estuary are rich in fish and invertebrates, a food source for waterbirds and shorebirds.

Though most species can be seen in various different habitat types, some are more likely viewing sites than others. Loons, Grebes, and Cormorants can be seen along the river and in bays. Cormorants also frequent the Baie des Cochons salt marsh, as do Bitterns, Great Blue Herons, and Night Herons.

Canada Geese and Snow Geese stop in the park on their spring and autumn migrations, as do several species of duck, such as the Common Eider. Wild and rare in densely populated areas, Black Ducks nest in marshes and ponds, also inhabited by northern pintails and Green-Winged Teals.

Shorebirds, as the term suggests, abound on shores, beaches, and bays. Plovers and Sandpipers are common sights, as are Gulls, Kittiwakes, and Double-Crested Cormorants. There are also at least two known Black Guillemot nesting sites in the park, and at least one more nearby.

■ Common Eider

There are more Common Eiders in Parc national du Bic than all other duck species combined, especially between May and August. Visitors wanting to see these flocks should plan their visit accordingly.

The Origin of the Name "Eider"

The word "eider" comes from the Icelandic word *aedhar*. An eiderdown quilt is one made from the soft down gathered from eider nests.

Île Bicquette, off the park's shore, houses 10,000 nests, making it the largest eider nesting site in the Gulf of St. Lawrence. The Canadian Wildlife Service, which owns the island, manages its protection as well as the down harvest: the ducks' famous down is gathered from abandoned nests and sold in Europe and Japan as an insulating material for clothes and sleeping bags.

The Common Eider, whose scientific name *Somateria mollissima* means "softest woolen body," is the largest duck in North America. This familiar bird of nordic coasts frequents all of Québec's seashores, where it feeds on mussels, periwinkles, and seaweed.

The Common Eider arrives in early April, congregating around Île Bicquette and its reefs. It can also be seen on the islets in Havre du Bic and Anse à l'Orignal.

Mating takes place between mid-April and May. The ducklings hatch in early June and are soon hurried into the water, but in the meantime, Gulls hunting in packs catch many of them.

In Parc national du Bic, Anse à l'Orignal is the eiders' favourite site for raising their ducklings. Many groups of adults and ducklings can be easily seen in the park's bays and coves.

■ Barrow's Goldeneye

This diving duck's fragmentary distribution through North America and Iceland raises concern over hunting and logging in its breeding sites.

According to the Canadian Wildlife Service, there are no more than 4,500 Barrow's Goldeneyes in eastern Canada. An estimated 10% stop in Parc national du Bic in autumn, mainly in Baie du Ha! Ha!.

■ Nelson's Sharp-Tailed Sparrow

Three quarters of this North American songbird's population nests in Canada. In Québec, this species is classified as likely to be classified as threatened or vulnerable because of the small number and area of protected nesting sites.

In Québec, Nelson's Sharp-Tailed Sparrow usually nests near brackish or salt marshes. Some individuals have recently been observed in Parc national du Bic, in the Havre-du-Bic sector.

■ Birds of Prey

The variety of habitats and the strong relief make the park an attractive home for birds of prey. Ospreys fly over the shore and salt marshes looking for prey, while Merlins are frequently spotted on Île Ronde and taking advantage of the good view from Mont Chocolat.

In the late 1980s, the Peregrine Falcon was successfully reintroduced to Parc national du Bic. Broods and flying falconets have been seen.

While Parc national du Bic is chiefly associated with seabirds, observing birds of prey can offer some pleasant surprises. The best place to spot them is the Raoul-Roy lookout. This lookout is named for a popular songwriter from Saint-Fabien-sur-Mer and owner of the town's Centre

When to Watch Wildlife

Species	Access	Period	Chances*
Harbour seal	The tide governs the presence of seals in the various areas of the park. When the tide is high enough to give seals access to boulders off Pointe aux Épinettes or the Rioux farm, these are the best spots. If the tide is too low here, they can be seen from the beaches at Anse aux Bouleaux Ouest and Anse aux Bouleaux Est, or on Récif à l'Orignal.	From ice breakup to mid-July	Occasional
		Mid-July to mid-September	Certain
		Mid-September to freeze-up	Occasional
Grey seal		Mid-July to late September	Occasional
Common Eider	All bays and coves of the park. Anse à l'Orignal is the best spot to see nesting eiders.	Early April to late June	Certain
		July to late August	Occasional

Birds of prey	The Raoul-Roy lookout is the best spot to see birds of prey during their spring migration.	April to late June	Certain
White-tailed deer	Throughout the park. Best locations: Pointe aux Épinettes salt marsh, fields, and near the Rivière-du-Sud-Ouest and Rioux campgrounds.	Spring and autumn Summer	Certain Occasional

* The chances of observing wildlife depend on local conditions—the tide schedule and weather, such as strong winds, fog and rain, all influence sightings.

Note: Seal-watching expeditions to the reef southwest of Île du Bic are certain to see seals between June and mid-September.

d'art Le Pirate, one of the best known concert venues in eastern Québec, which held concerts by Félix Leclerc, Gilles Vigneault, Claude Léveillée, Claude Gauthier, and Pauline Julien. This lookout, west of Pic Champlain, can be reached from the road to Saint-Fabien-sur-Mer.

The almost constant presence of rising air currents along the rock faces allows bird of prey to fly long distances with minimal effort. This concentrates birds of prey in a relatively narrow corridor near the lookout, a boon to bird-watchers.

From April to late June, visitors can see most of Québec's bird of prey species here, since this exceptional site is located on a migration corridor. Most birds of prey—vultures, hawks, eagles, and falcons—fly south for the winter and return in spring to breed.

Every spring since 1982, in collaboration with Parc national du Bic, the members of the Club d'ornithologie du Bas-Saint-Laurent have inventoried the species of birds of prey observed from the Saint-Fabien-sur-Mer lookout. Of the fifteen represented species, the Red-Tailed Hawk and Sharp-Shinned Hawk are the most common. Pic Champlain is also one of the best observation sites for the Golden Eagle in Québec.

Like the Red-Tailed Hawk, Broad-Winged and Rough-Legged Hawks fly over fields and plains looking for small mammals; Northern Goshawks and Northern Harriers can also be spotted. Among the small birds of prey, three species of falcons can be seen: the successfully reintroduced Peregrine Falcon, the Merlin, and the American Kestrel.

Formerly quite rare, the Turkey Vulture is seen more and more often. It is thought to nest near the park, in the cliff opposite the Rivière-du-Sud-Ouest Information Kiosk, south of Route 132.

During the spring migration, many birds of prey fly 35km across the estuary between the park and the Côte-Nord region. Most are Bald Eagles.

Peregrine Falcon: The Peregrine Falcon is officially a vulnerable species in Québec. The catastrophic decline in this bird's numbers in the mid-20th century was caused by the use of the pesticide DDT.

In the late 1980s, the Canadian Wildlife Service and the Ministère du Loisir, de la Chasse et de la Pêche participated in a reintroduction program for the Peregrine Falcon, releasing 15 falconets in Parc national du Bic.

Following the reintroduction, nests have regularly been reported in the cliff south of Baie du Ha! Ha!; one was found 80m up the cliff.

Overview of Activities

The theme of the park's interpretive program, *A Legacy of the Sea*, is very present: nearly all the park's activities are related to the sea or seashore. There are numerous ways to explore the estuarine jewel that is Parc national du Bic.

Discovery Activities

Before beginning your exploration of the park, a stop at the Discovery and Visitors Centre is highly recommended, even if you do nothing but see the permanent exhibit *A Legacy of the Sea*. Numerous audiovisual presentations give an instant overview of the park.

Park warden naturalists help visitors to discover the many faces of the park: the hard lives of shore creatures, the constantly evolving landscapes, and the history of human occupation.

Theatrical presentations on the history of the region are offered, while special activities and talks reveal the rich fauna, flora, and geology of the areas. To follow the footsteps of Aboriginal peoples through the park, explore the 200m-long Sentier Archéologique. Six interpretive panels take you on a 2,500-year journey through time. Other panels throughout the park provide interesting information about the landscape, the fauna, the flora, and the history of its various sectors.

Summer Pleasures

■ Minibus Tour

During the summer, a minibus tour gives you the chance to discover the landscape, history, and legends of the park. The route offers views of Île aux Amours, Cap Caribou, and Pointe aux Épinettes. A stop at the Pic-Champlain lookout (346m) reveals stunning panoramas. A motorized shuttle from the Pic-Champlain parking lot to the lookout, without the rest of the tour, is also available.

■ Sea Kayaking

For an especially spectacular encounter with seals and seabirds, nothing beats a sea kayak expedition. Of course, you must still keep your distance to prevent them from becoming alarmed. Floating on the water in the middle of the estuary is an amazing experience, and a sunset excursion is truly majestic.

■ Inflatable Boat Excursions

The well-known Zodiac inflatable boat offers safety and comfort during the thrilling experience of exploring the estuary. Guided tours visit Île Bicquette and Île du Bic, giving visitors the chance to learn about the maritime history of the area.

■ Yachting

To protect the seals and birds from disturbance, all craft are prohibited from entering most of the Anse à l'Orignal marine preservation area. However, pleasure craft are welcome in several attractive areas such as Baie du Ha! Ha! and Havre du Bic. In the latter, pleasure boaters have access to a launching ramp and a mooring basin.

■ Cycling

Bike paths cross numerous habitats from shoreline to grasslands. The 15km of paths are not intended so much for cycling enthusiasts who want to spend the whole day riding as for visitors who want another way to discover the beauty of the park. Several of the paths are ideal for cycling with children.

Starting point: The Discovery and Visitors Centre in the middle of the park is the starting point for the bicycle paths.

Le Portage

Length: 4km
Time: 15min
Level: easy

This path gives an excellent view of the Lower St. Lawrence's typical harmony of mountain plateaus and peaks. This path, mainly running through fields, has a stop with a good view of Anse à l'Orignal.

Near the end of the bicycle path, you'll cross a 0.5-km pedestrian path leading to Mont Chocolat. It's worth parking your bike and having a look at the rockside shelters and the view of Baie des Cochons.

A few decades ago, a forest fire stripped the mountain bare. Inspired by its charred brown colour and its shape resembling the well-known Cherry Blossom chocolate candies, young vacationers named it Mont Chocolat.

La Grève

Length: 5km
Time: 25min
Level: easy

The trail first runs along Baie du Ha! Ha!, with its intoxicating sea breeze, especially with fog or a west wind. Wild roses along the trail also add their delightful perfume.

The trail then passes the Rioux farm, where four generations raised crops and livestock, fished, and logged. It then goes past a tracery of coves and rock bars as far as the tip of Cap à l'Orignal. Legend has it that at this spot, a moose (*orignal*) pursued by hunters threw itself into the sea, giving its name to the point.

La Coulée-à-Blanchette

Length: 5km
Time: 45min
Level: intermediate

This peaceful trail runs through a forest landscape dominated to the east by Pic Champlain. Near the end of the trail, you'll cross Lac à Crapauds, an unusual little rectangular lake bordered by very thick floating vegetation.

The route ends at Anse à Capelans, with its little beach, an ideal place to dismount and rest awhile.

Nearby, a walking path follows the shores of Îlet au Flacon. This name, "bottle islet," comes from the 1749 wreck of a French ship loaded with wine and brandy. Only part of the cargo was recovered, and bottles of liquor may have turned up on the island's shoals.

La Pointe-aux-Épinettes

Length: 0.7km
Time: 5min
Level: easy

This trail leads to Pointe aux Épinettes, where a lookout gives an excellent view of the salt marsh. Seals can often be seen at high tide. In summer, a park warden naturalist helps visitors discover the shoreline.

Tip

If you don't have much time but you still want a good overview of the park by bicycle, try taking the La Grève trail round trip from the Discovery and Visitors Centre. If you still have some time after, start along the Le Portage trail, then turn off onto the La Pointe-aux-Épinettes trail, following it to Pointe aux Épinettes.

■ Hiking

It's not every day you have the chance to walk along the beach, much less on the majestic St. Lawrence estuary. In Parc national du Bic, however, there are areas accessible on foot along the whole shore. Check tide tables; some areas can become difficult at high tide.

The park offers 25km of trails. The Saint-Fabien and Pic-Champlain lookouts are choice locations for watching the spring birds of prey, and a visit to Anse à l'Orignal is a must for the seals and eiders.

The trails below leave from the Discovery and Visitors Centre.

··· Cap-à-l'Orignal sector

Le Contrebandier

Length: 1.1km
Time: 20min
Level: easy
Departure: Discovery and Visitors Centre or Rioux farm

This centre runs past ancient marine terraces. Leaving the forest, the bracing sea air wafts from Anse à Mouille-Cul. This trail gets its unusual name from the Prohibition period, when bootleggers arrived in boats to collect cargoes of contraband whisky brought by sea from Saint-Pierre-et-Miquelon. As they had to tie up silently, they sometimes jumped into waist-deep water to push their boats up to the shore. The discovery activity on this subject holds many surprises for visitors.

Le Miquelon

Length: 1.9km
Time: 40min
Level: easy
Departure: Discovery and Visitors Centre or Rioux farm

This trail gives access to the Wootton and Feindel cabins. Originally a house and a barn, these two old buildings stand on what the locals call the *terre du nord*, which was both farmed and logged. In the mountains, the mysterious forest makes for a unique hiking experience.

Les Escaliers

Length: 0.9km
Time: 30min
Level: difficult
Departure: Discovery and Visitors Centre or Rioux farm

This is a shortcut between the Le Scoggan and Le Miquelon trails, running steeply up the side of Montagne à Michaud.

La Pinède

Length: 1km
Time: 35min
Level: difficult
Departure: Discovery and Visitors Centre or Rioux farm

Amid the lovely scent of the jack pine woods, this trail looks over the estuary to the north and Anse à l'Orignal to the east.

Le Scoggan

Length: 2.9km
Time: 1h30
Level: intermediate
Departure: Discovery and Visitors Centre or Rioux farm

This trail was named in honour of prominent Canadian botanist Homer J. Scoggan, who cata-logued some 710 species of vascular plants in the park during the 1940s. The trail that bears his name crosses Montagne à Michaud and runs along the crests from east to west. At your feet is a rugged landscape over Baie du Ha! Ha!. From the trail's two lookouts, Les Murailles and Pic Champlain rise in the distance in all their splendour.

Sentier Archéologique

Length: 0.2km
Time: 20min
Level: easy
Departure: Discovery and Visitors Centre or Rioux farm

Along this trail, six interpretive panels reveal the history of the land and the Aboriginal people who once lived here.

Le Chemin-du-Nord

Length: 2.2km
Time: 50min
Level: easy
Departure: Rioux farm

This trail is the perfect way to take in the charms of the seaside. Seals are a common site from near the Rioux farm at high tide, while the scent of wild rosebushes wafts near Anse à Wilson.

Parc national du Bic – Overview of Activities – Summer Pleasures

This trail connects with the Le Miquelon trail near the Wootton and Feindel cabins. These two old buildings testify to the farmers, loggers, hunters, and fishers who once lived here, before the area became a vacation site in the 1920s.

The land and the two buildings, a house and barn, once belonged to the Michaud family. After several sales and an inheritance, the house came into the hands of the wife of a Captain T. A. Wootton. The barn, for its part, was sold and turned into a cottage, eventually becoming the property of a certain Colonel Lyman's daughter, who married a Dr. Feindel.

To the north is found the Lyman estate, once part of the same land. It features five buildings and a unique colonial revival cottage.

⋯ Central sector

La Colonie

Length: 2.7km
Time: 1h
Level: easy

Running through fields and up a small hill, this short trail links the La Citadelle trail with the Rioux farm sector. It crosses one of Québec's first summer camps, Cap à l'Orignal, founded in 1948 by Father Louis-Georges Lamontagne and still in operation today. It also leads to the Discovery and Visitors Centre.

Le Pic-Champlain

Length: 3km
Time: 1h30
Level: intermediate
Departure: Discovery and Visitors Centre

During his first voyage in 1603, Samuel de Champlain used this mountain as a landmark on a navigational chart, hence its name. Technology marches on, but the mountain still serves as a guide today—it now houses a communications tower.

The trail rises gradually to the peak, the park's highest point (346m). A lookout gives a 180° view over much of the area; the beauty of the relief and the lush vegetation make this the most remarkable panorama in the park.

A minibus runs from the Pic-Champlain parking lot to the lookout. Visitors can use it either as a round trip or to go one way up or down.

Les Murailles

Length: 4.5km
Time: 2h
Level: difficult
Departure: Raoul-Roy lookout parking lot

This trail takes you between land and sky along a rocky crest, with a stunning view of the estuary and the Appalachian countryside. It also gives access to the Raoul-Roy lookout, the best place to view birds of prey in spring. The trail starts with a hard climb up a series of stairs, but becomes much smoother as you approach the lookout.

··· La Citadelle sector

La Citadelle

Length: 4.6km
Time: 1h50
Level: intermediate
Departure: Discovery and Visitors Centre and Rivière-du-Sud-Ouest parking lot

This trail follows an old logging trail from the time when locals cut down small amounts of wood for their own use. The flora is lush and varied.

··· Cap-Caribou and Île-aux-Amours sectors

Les Anses

Length: 1.4km
Time: 25min
Level: intermediate
Departure: Île-aux-Amours parking lot

On this walk, which runs partly through the forest and partly along the coast, you'll discover the diversity of the seashore and a remarkable beach. This little-used trail leads to Anse aux Bouleaux Est and Anse aux Bouleaux Ouest, the latter being one of the best places to watch seals at low tide.

When the tide is out, a drying sand bank leads to Île aux Amours, which you can tour on foot. There are a couple of stories about where this island got its name. According to one local legend, young lovebirds would walk out to this island together, where the rising tide would give them a few hours of solitude.

Another story has it that in the summer of 1938, two fishermen looking out at the estuary through binoculars saw naked women on the island. The story raced through town, and while the men talked about it with amusement, the local Catholic ladies' auxiliaries were so scandalized that they woke up the Bishop of Rimouski in the middle of the night! The village priests investigated, but found no trace of the mysterious women...

Tip

For a quick visit, take the shuttle to the Pic-Champlain lookout for a superb view of the estuary with its bays and coves. For a superb sunset, visit Baie du Ha! Ha! or the Havre-du-Bic sector near the launching ramp.

Early risers should visit the salt marsh for the chance to see white-tailed deer. And if you'd like a quick hour-long stroll, take Chemin-du-Nord to admire a postcard-perfect scene amid the heavenly scent of wild roses.

Winter Pleasures

Few people know that Parc national du Bic is open in winter. Accordingly, there's no more peaceful spot to practise your favourite sports.

The main departure point is the Rivière-du-Sud-Ouest Information Kiosk on Route 132. The Information Kiosk offers the usual services: information on activities and lodging, washrooms, outdoors boutique, and equipment rentals (snowshoes and kick sleds).

Hikers have two heated warming huts at their disposal: Le Porc-épic at 900m and Le Pékan at 4.5km.

■ Backcountry Skiing

Skiers used to running single file down neatly traced paths are in for a new experience—the 20km of trails are marked, but not groomed, offering intimate contact with the grand landscapes of the forest and coast.

■ Snowshoes

Snowshoeing past a majestic view of the St. Lawrence estuary is a truly remarkable experience. Novices and adventurers have access to 30km of marked trails.

■ Snow Hiking

Parc national du Bic now offers 5km of trails for snow hiking. Hikers can also enjoy a novel experience by renting a kick sled at the Information Kiosk.

■ Trails

Sentier Multifonctionnel
(Multi-Use Trail)

Length: 4.5km
Level: easy
Departure: Rivière-du-Sud-Ouest
Information Kiosk
Activities: cross-country skiing,
snowshoeing, or hiking

This trail crosses through the
heart of the park to the Le
Pékan warming hut. Warmed
by a woodstove, this shelter is
a pleasant place to stop for a
snack and a hot chocolate.

La Pointe-aux-Épinettes

Length: 0.7km
Level: easy
Departure: Sentier Multifonctionnel
Activities: cross-country skiing,
snowshoeing, or hiking

Branching off from Sentier
Multifonctionnel, this trail leads
to Pointe aux Épinettes, offering
a lovely view of the river ice
pack and Anse à l'Orignal.

Le Contrebandier

Length: 1km
Level: easy
Departure: Chemin-du-Nord
Activities: cross-country skiing or
snowshoeing

Le Contrebandier splits off from
the left side of the Chemin-du-
Nord trail. It runs along Anse à
Mouille-Cul for most of its length,
overlooking the ice pack.

La Citadelle

Length: 5.7km
Level: intermediate
Departure: Rivière-du-Sud-Ouest
bridge
Activities: cross-country skiing or
snowshoeing

This trail through the forest
passes through the traces of
a logging camp. Some slopes
are steep enough that skiers
need to use a herringbone step
to climb them. This is a one-
way trail, returning via Sentier
Multifonctionnel.

La Coulée-à-Blanchette

Length: 4.5km
Level: intermediate
Departure: La Citadelle trail
Activities: cross-country skiing or
snowshoeing

This trail runs along a summer
bicycle path through the forest
to Îlet au Flacon. As a western
extension of La Citadelle trail,
it shares that trail's rises and
descents.

Parc national du Bic - Overview of Activities - Winter Pleasures

Le Chemin-du-Nord

Length: 4km
Level: easy
Departure: Le Pékan warming hut
Activities: cross-country skiing or snowshoeing

After resting for a while at the Le Pékan warming hut and enjoying La Colonie trail, take Chemin-du-Nord trail along the shore of Anse à l'Orignal. Take a break on the balcony of the Wootton and Feindel cabins, then head out to the end of Cap à l'Orignal.

La Pinède

Length: 2km
Level: intermediate
Departure: Chemin-du-Nord or Le Scoggan
Activity: snowshoeing

On Montagne à Michaud, keep an eye out for trees stripped by porcupines and other signs of these rodents' presence. The steep trail leads to two lookouts, with great views of Anse à l'Orignal and Anse à Mouille-Cul.

Les Anses

Length: 2.2km
Level: intermediate
Departure: Sentier Multifonctionnel or Porc-Épic warming hut
Activity: snowshoeing

This aptly named trail runs along Anse aux Bouleaux Ouest and Anse aux Bouleaux Est, near igloos, yurts, and the Porc-Épic warming hut. The loop ends in a climb up Cap Caribou; be sure to save some energy for this short but brisk climb.

Le Pic-Champlain

Length: 7.2km
Level: difficult
Departure: Rivière-du-Sud-Ouest Information Kiosk
Activity: snowshoeing

You need strong legs to make it to the Pic-Champlain lookout and enjoy the magnificent view, especially if you choose to start via La Citadelle trail. After following the trail, you must climb the mountain—in all, the makings of a good, full day out.

Important!

All the distance measurements are based on a one-way trip. For the length of a whole trip, don't forget to add up the length of each segment. For example, if you want to go from the Rivière-du-Sud-Ouest visitors centre to Cap à l'Orignal, you'll need to take both Sentier Multifonctionnel (4.5km) and Chemin-du-Nord (4km), a total of 8.5km. For a round trip, this makes 17km.

Practical Information

Lodging

■ Camping

In summer, Parc national du Bic offers three campgrounds with more than 200 sites. Most of these are in the Rivière-du-Sud-Ouest campground, one of the first campsites created in 1950 for visitors to the region.

Since the park first opened, this campground has been controversial because of the noise from the nearby highway and railway. However, it would have been impossible to set up a campground with a similar size and services well inside a relatively small park such as Le Bic without severe consequences for the natural habitat.

The Rioux campground, near the Rioux farm, offers 50 unserviced campsites. It is located in a former agricultural area; over the years, the returning vegetation has provided the campsites with extra privacy. The campsites on the western side offer beautiful views of Baie du Ha! Ha!.

La Coulée campground, near the shore, has just eight campsites on platforms surrounded by forest. This isolated, peaceful campground, about 1km from the Îlet-au-Flacon parking lot, can be accessed on foot or by bicycle via La Coulée-à-Blanchette trail. It can also be reached by sea kayak from the estuary.

Camping season runs from mid-May to early October. Winter camping is offered in the Île-aux-Amours and Pointe-aux-Épinettes sectors. For safety reasons, at least two adults per sector are required.

■ In a Yurt

What in the world is a yurt? It's a circular felt tent, the traditional dwelling of the nomads of Central Asia. Seven four-person yurts are available for rent in the Île-aux-Amours sector. The tents, 6m in diameter, have larch floors and are furnished and adapted for comfort.

They are equipped with a wood stove, a refrigerator, propane lamps, and a complete set of cooking equipment. Large windows provide a view of the estuary. At night, you can watch the stars through a clear dome at the peak of the roof. Firepits and picnic tables are available nearby, and there is shore access.

■ Shelter

Less than 1km from the Rivière-du-Sud-Ouest Information Kiosk, the Le Harfang shelter sleeps up to eight people in its four modern bedrooms. Available early September to mid-June.

■ Quinzees

Also less than 1km from the Rivière-du-Sud-Ouest Information Kiosk, four quinzees sleep up to four people each. These snow houses are similar to igloos, but are built from a mound of snow which is hollowed out from the inside, resulting in excellent insulation—the inside temperature is no colder than 0°C. With sleeping bags rated down to −20°C available for rent, a polar fleece blanket, a warming hut nearby, and a fire pit right outside, the experience is actually very comfortable. As for winter camping, at least two adults must be staying in the sector, for safety reasons.

■ Camp Cap à l'Orignal

This summer camp at the heart of the park offers young people a wide variety of outdoor activities such as hikes and cycling. Young adventurers also have a chance to discover the park's seals and seabirds.

Stays of 7 to 28 days are offered, from mid-May to the third week of September. For more details, contact the company that runs the camp *(www.capalorignal. com)*.

■ Nearby

Visitors can also stay in one of the two villages near the park, Saint-Fabien and Le Bic. Year-round or nearly so, both have numerous charming and comfortable inns, ideal for an inexpensive stay while visiting the park.

Renting a cabin is also a great way to enjoy a pleasant and affordable stay right next to the park. Even the delightful inns with full board in Le Bic generally offer good prices for the region.

Dining

■ Rioux Farm

The Rioux farm has a snack bar and vending machines.

■ Nearby

The village of Le Bic offers a good choice of restaurants. For a relaxing bistro atmosphere and affordable prices, try Chez Saint-Pierre *(129 Rue Mont-St-Louis, ☎418-736-5051)*, which serves tasty dishes and an interesting selection of beers. For a more innovative culinary experience, try Auberge du Mange Grenouille *(148 Rue Ste-Cécile, ☎418-736-5656)*.

Services

■ Rivière-du-Sud-Ouest Information Kiosk

This Information Kiosk includes a bicycle rental desk, a convenience store, and a small Boutique Nature store selling quality clothing and gifts from the Parcs Québec collection.

■ Rioux Farm

The Boutique Nature shop at the Rioux farm offers artworks and crafts from local artists as well as Parcs Québec souvenirs.

Nearby

A trip through the nearby villages reveals the seaside atmosphere of the estuary, enhanced by beautiful, well-preserved ancestral houses.

Saint-Fabien

The capelin "scull" on the beaches of Saint-Fabien in May, crawling out of the water to spawn on the shore. Even if you don't arrive in season to witness this phenomenon, you'll find this village and the nearby coast (Saint-Fabien-sur-Mer) quite charming, with its cliff-side summer houses. Nearby, the agricultural prosperity that brought settlers to this land nearly two hundred years ago continues in cultivated fields and peat bogs.

The village is easy to take in by bicycle. A stop at an art gallery or a show at the local theatre are good ways to spend your time, as is a visit to the old brick-clad church, skilfully restored 30 years ago.

One unique excursion is a visit to the old Barytine mine. Take Chemin de la Mine; a guide is on site every day from June to September.

Le Bic

Farther east, the village of Le Bic attracts visitors with its impressive landscape, pretty streets, art gallery, and artisanal bakery. We suggest parking your car at the centre of town and exploring on foot.

Besides the picturesque, well-preserved old houses, the main architectural attraction is the impressive neo-Gothic Sainte-Cécile du Bic church, its facade dominating the harbour.

A play is a pleasant diversion in summer, while golfers have two courses to practise their pastime.

Pointe-au-Père

The Pointe-au-Père Lighthouse National Historic Site of Canada, about 30km east of Parc national du Bic, is one of Canada's highest lighthouses, and was once one of the country's most important navigational aid centres.

Saguenay–St. Lawrence Marine Park

While travelling through the Bas-Saint-Laurent region to reach Parc national du Bic, you will run past the majestic St. Lawrence River, home to Québec's first marine conservation area. This 1,245km^2 preserve is jointly managed by the Québec government (Parcs Québec, Sépaq) and the federal government (Parks Canada). Its mandate is to conserve the species and ecosystems of part of the St. Lawrence River and Fjord du Saguenay. To find out more about discovering the riches of the St. Lawrence, visit one of the two information and reception centres in Rivière-du-Loup and Trois-Pistoles, or visit the Web site at *www.parcmarin. qc.ca*.

Parc national du Bic and its surroundings have everything you could want for an exciting long weekend or a wonderful vacation.

Tourisme Bas-Saint-Laurent
☎ 418-867-3015 or 1-800-563-5268
www.tourismebas-st-laurent.com

PARC NATIONAL DE LA GASPÉSIE

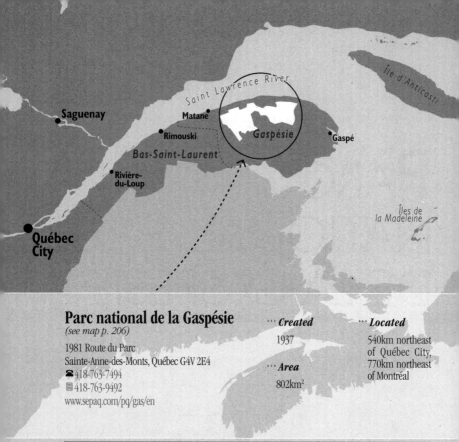

Parc national de la Gaspésie
(see map p. 206)

1981 Route du Parc
Sainte-Anne-des-Monts, Québec G4V 2E4
☎ 418-763-7494
🖷 418-763-9492
www.sepaq.com/pq/gas/en

··· **Created**
1937

··· **Area**
802km²

··· **Located**
540km northeast
of Québec City,
770km northeast
of Montréal

Our Highlights

Parc national de la Gaspésie's must-see highlights begin with the mountains themselves. Between the Chic-Chocs and McGerrigle ranges, the **highway through the park** affords a great overview of this exceptional alpine environment. In the heart of the mountains, **Gîte du Mont-Albert** is a perfect stop for a delicious meal and comfortable rest in vertiginous surroundings.

The trails into the **high mountain area**, especially those to Mont Albert and Mont Jacques-Cartier, lead to landscapes unique in Québec: high plateaus where the forest gives way to tundra. Here, you may see a few members of the only herd of caribou south of the St. Lawrence River, the endangered woodland caribou.

The **hiking** and **cross-country skiing** is amazing, whether you set out to conquer the high plateaus or explore the gentler terrain of the valleys.

Rivière Sainte-Anne and its **salmon pools** are another choice destination, as is **Lac Cascapédia** with its gently curving shores bounded by endless forest.

Visiting Time

⋯ *One hour*

An hour is not much time at all, but it is enough to get a good view and develop the yen to come back for a longer visit. In an hour, you can drive through the whole park on the main highway, which crosses it north to south between the largest mountain chains. Take a quarter hour to get out of the car and visit the Discovery and Visitors Centre, located near Gîte du Mont-Albert, and its permanent exhibit called *A Sea of Mountains in the Heart of the Gaspé Peninsula*. You'll get a glimpse of the many faces of the mountaintops.

⋯ *A half day*

A half-day visit will give you more of an opportunity to get a feel for the park. A good option is to park at the Discovery and Visitors Centre and explore one of the numerous trails that depart from Gîte du Mont-Albert. The La Saillie, La Lucarne, and Chute-Sainte-Anne trails are short walks of less than two hours. Once your hike (on foot or cross-country skis, depending on the season) is done, top off your day with a cocktail at the Gîte du Mont-Albert bar while gazing at the unique scenery of the Chic-Chocs mountains.

⋯ *One day or longer*

Warning: once you wake up in the enchanting Parc national de la Gaspésie, you may never want to leave. The hiking opportunities in any season are innumerable and there's something for any level of hiker. You can start with short hikes and work your way up to tackling a 1,000m climb. For those who simply want to relax, Lac Cascapédia is the perfect place to lounge in a landscape right out of a postcard.

Gîte du Mont-Albert is a great value with its comfortable rooms and splendid dining. Cabins are also available for greater privacy, while independent camping and long-distance hiking are other ways to discover the park over a period of several days.

It is impossible to overstate the grandeur of Parc national de la Gaspésie, the majestic Appalachian Mountains' last bastion before they plunge into the Gulf of St. Lawrence. A few images: a sea of mountain summits piercing the clouds a kilometre above you; the only herd of caribou south of the St. Lawrence; narrow paths snaking through the landscapes, yours to explore on foot in the summer or on snowshoes or skis in the winter.

Some History

Human Habitation

■ The Mi'kmaq

When the first Europeans arrived, the Gaspé peninsula was already home to the Mi'kmaq, who journeyed along the natural highways of rivers and valleys including the Rivière Sainte-Anne valley. In the 16th century, the Mi'kmaq nation's population was about 20,000 strong in a territory covering the present-day provinces of Nova Scotia, New Brunswick and Prince Edward Island, making them the dominant aboriginal nation in Atlantic Canada.

The hunter-gatherer Mi'kmaq were also excellent fishers and built very durable bark canoes. They lived in coastal villages in the summer, returning to inland quarters in the winter to benefit from better hunting. Numerous place names in Gaspé, including the Chic-Chocs mountains, come from the Mi'kmaq language. Today, some 5,000 Mi'kmaq live in Québec.

■ The Park's First Explorers

The first people to do any in-depth exploring of Parc national de la Gaspésie's current territory were scientists. A number of geologists studied the future park intensely in the 19th century, hoping to uncover the secrets of this unique environment. Guided by the coast's inhabitants, these adventurers trekked along river valleys to reach new horizons. Explorers in the purest sense of the word, these passionate naturalists lived off game and fish as they probed the mountains.

Geologist William Logan and his expedition penetrated the interior of the Gaspé Peninsula in 1844. They traced Rivière Cap-Chat and climbed the mountain now named for Logan before returning via Rivière Cascapédia. The next year, Logan's assistant and fellow geologist Alexander Murray returned to explore Rivière Sainte-Anne. He also scaled a tall peak which he named Mont Albert in honour of Prince Albert, Queen Victoria's husband.

A third geologist, James Richardson, undertook another expedition a few years later in 1857. He and his team explored Rivière Madeleine, Mont Jacques-Cartier, and Mont Richardson, named in honour of this geologist.

Besides these pioneers, a generation of other scientists— botanists, biologists, cartographers, and geographers— came to the region to add to the work the geologists had begun. Starting in 1800, the region was surveyed in turn by John Macoun, Albert Peter Low, and R. Hugh Ells. The latter, a member of the Geological Survey of Canada, was the first to return with photographs of the region, and he also mapped Lac Cascapédia. For their part, Macoun and Low explored the high peaks and identified hundreds of plant species.

Between 1905 and 1923, Merritt Lyndon Fernald, an American botanist and Harvard professor, made four trips to the mountains of Gaspésie, bringing to light the

Military Presence in the Park

Between 1942 and 1945, the Canadian army ran a telecommunications station on the peak of Mont Jacques-Cartier, 1,270m above sea level. It abandoned the station after the Second World War, and the only traces that remain are concrete foundations and radio antennas.

unique flora living in the future Parc national de la Gaspésie.

Eminent Québec botanist Brother Marie-Victorin travelled to Gaspésie twice, in 1923 and 1940. Captivated by what he found there, he discussed the flora of the Chic-Chocs in his celebrated treatise, *Flore Laurentienne*. Other scientists, such as Father Louis-Marie Lalonde, Camille Gervais, and Harold William McGerrigle (who gave his name to a granite range in Gaspésie), would continue to explore the mysterious natural world of Gaspésie in the same period.

The Creation of the Park

Over time, the reputation of the area solidified as scientist after scientist returned from their expeditions in awe of the region's natural treasures. Accordingly, the idea of protecting this Eden from uncontrolled development was soon proposed. A world conservation movement had been born in the United States at the end of the 19th century with the creation of Yellowstone Park (1872), soon followed by Canada's Banff National Park (1885). In Québec, Parc de la Montagne-Tremblante (today Parc national du Mont-Tremblant) and Parc des Laurentides (today Réserve faunique des Laurentides) were created a decade later, in 1894 and 1895 respectively.

Accordingly, on April 14, 1937, the government of Premier Maurice Duplessis inaugurated Parc de la Gaspésie as Québec's third national park. Clear objectives were estab-

Exploitation of Natural Resources in the Park

In 1938, permission to cut down trees at least 50 years old in part of the park was granted indefinitely. A sawfly outbreak and the risk of forest fires justified this measure. Also, copper, silver, and zinc mines were opened in some parts of the park in the first few decades after it was created. In 1981, the park was finally designated a "conservation park," ensuring its complete protection under the new *Parks Act* of 1977.

lished: protecting Mont Albert and the Tabletop (today McGerrigle) range, the salmon of Rivière Sainte-Anne, and the caribou herd, and promoting tourism in Gaspésie. These four objectives still form the heart of the park's conservation mission.

In 1938, five buildings and the foundation of the future Gîte du Mont-Albert were built where the inn stands today. However, work was interrupted by the outbreak of the Second World War.

Gradually, trails spread through the preserve. In 1956, a highway across the peninsula from Sainte-Anne-des-Monts on the St. Lawrence to New Richmond on Chaleur Bay was built through the heart of Parc de la Gaspésie.

In 1950, Gîte du Mont-Albert opened its doors, and swiftly established itself as a star of the Québec tourism landscape. The first manager, Ms. Laurette Gagné, worked feverishly to run the establishment, as did chef Euclide Béland, who arrived in 1953. Though the Gîte had neither electricity nor telephone service in those days, ambitious projects were born, such as a cooking course given by the chef and sanctioned by the Institut de tourisme et d'hôtellerie du Québec.

On July 24, 1959, a massive forest fire devastated the park, burning more than 35km² of forest and threatening Gîte du Mont-Albert before changing direction. Other fires stormed the park in 1965 and 1968; more than a hundred men fought the 1968 fire for over a month.

Parc national de la Gaspésie - Some History - The Creation of the Park

The years 1984 and 1985 saw the construction of an interpretive centre and the creation of campgrounds. Later, in
1993, major renovations at Gîte du Mont-Albert added a
new building with 48 rooms. The inn retains its original
dining room, its reputation upheld to this day by a succession of excellent chefs.

The interpretive centre has recently been enlarged to
offer more services as the Discovery and Visitors Centre.
Located near Gîte du Mont-Albert, it presents a permanent exhibit, *A Sea of Mountains in the Heart of the Gaspé
Peninsula*, introducing visitors to the park and its natural
and historical heritage. The centre also offers a number
of services, including outdoor equipment rentals for items
such as snowshoes and cross-country skis.

Geography and Geology

Geography

Parc national de la Gaspésie is located in the northern
part of the long Appalachian mountain chain. This
chain extends thousands of kilometres from Alabama to
Newfoundland, making it the longest mountain chain in
eastern North America. The mountains of Gaspésie are the
highest mountains in Québec, except for the remote and
inaccessible Torngat Mountains near Ungava Bay on the
far northern border with Labrador.

The park is located in the portion of the Appalachians
known as Notre-Dame Mountains, and contains two

important ranges—the Chic-Choc Mountains and the McGerrigle Mountains.

With 25 summits over 1,000m in altitude, some merely 20km from the St. Lawrence River, the mountains do justice to the Mi'kmaq origin of their name: *sigôg*, "impenetrable barriers." Though not in the league of western Canada's Rocky Mountains, these are rocky giants whose highest peak, Mont Jacques-Cartier in the McGerrigle range, reaches 1,270m—Québec's second-highest mountain. The McGerrigle range alone includes 7 of the province's 10 highest mountains. This loftiness that so typifies the park creates landscapes reminiscent of Québec's Far North, with flora and fauna to match: caribou, arctic and alpine plants, and the like.

The highway that crosses the park from north to south follows the course of Rivière Sainte-Anne. A natural access route, the glacial valley of Rivière Sainte-Anne has always been the gateway to the region. This river divides the two major ranges, the Chic-Chocs and the McGerrigle range. Located less than 10km on either side of the highway, the mountains exceed 1,000m in altitude. Mont Richardson, Mont Joseph-Fortin, and Mont Albert with its southern and northern summits, are majestic sights, their peaks often lost in the clouds. Seen from the mountainsides, cars on the highway below look smaller than toys.

Geology

The whole Gaspésie region, like the park of the same name, was created by the accumulation of sediment on the sea floor. A series of uplifts in the earth's crust, followed by powerful folding, created the high ridges that we see today. Successive glaciations gave the area its current appearance. The erosion of the glaciers acted like a huge sheet of sandpaper, rounding off the mountain peaks and giving them their truncated appearance like a pyramid without a tip.

The Chic-Chocs range is estimated to be 600 million years old. The mountains consist mainly of volcanic and sedimentary rocks. However, Mont Albert's unique orange colour derives from serpentine, a rock usually found under the ocean. As the Chic-Chocs were created, this mountain rose from deep within the earth's crust before being exposed by hundreds of millions of years of erosion and glaciation.

The uplift of the earth's crust and periods of intense erosion uncovered numerous granite blocks in the McGerrigle range, a mere youngster at 380 million years old. The McGerrigle Mountains are mainly composed of granite created by the pressure and heat of molten rock infiltrating the crust from the bowels of the earth. The metamorphic rock surrounding the McGerrigle Mountains can be seen in the area of Mont Richardson and Lac aux Américains.

Features of the Park

The Mountains

Though smaller than the Rockies in the west of North America, the Appalachians are the most important mountain chain in eastern North America. The ranges protected by Parc national de la Gaspésie belong to this vast cordillera, beginning in Alabama and reaching as far as Newfoundland, after crossing under the Gulf of St. Lawrence.

The Chic-Chocs range is located west of Rivière Sainte-Anne. It runs parallel to the St. Lawrence, and is about 90km long and 10km wide. Seen from the north, dizzying rock walls drop sharply away, while to the south, the terrain is less rugged and descends gently. The tallest mountain in the Chic-Chocs, Mont Albert, is 1,154m high.

East of Rivière Sainte-Anne, the McGerrigle Mountains (formerly the Tabletop Mountains) can be recognized by their rounded peaks. Smaller than its neighbour, the Chic-Chocs, the McGerrigle range is about 18km by 6km, but its highest peak, Mont Jacques-Cartier, climbs 1,270m above sea level.

Climate

The climate of Parc national de la Gaspésie is intimately linked to its mountains. Although the park is within the temperate humid continental climate zone, this change to tundra with altitude.

Being able to start from a lush valley and reach a barren rock summit the same day is an extraordinary experience. This climate variation in such a small territory, in the southern half of the province no less, is unique in Québec.

The contrast between the icy winters and the July heat is more pronounced in the park than on the riverside, where the St. Lawrence moderates the climate. However, the presence of the river causes some of the most abundant snowfall in Québec. The province's most ardent snow lovers flock to the Chic-Chocs for wilderness skiing in a landscape where there are no lifts or marked trails to mar the infinite whiteness.

Annual totals of more than 7m of snow are not uncommon. On Mont Logan, for example, snow covers the summit

Avalanches

Copious snow, steep rock walls, and violent winds that compact the snow create perfect conditions for an avalanche. But often the trigger is someone practising a winter sport. A snowshoer, skier, or snowboarder at the wrong place at the wrong time can dislodge a snow slab and cause an avalanche.

The Centre d'avalanche de la Haute-Gaspésie at Sainte-Anne-des-Monts (*www.centreavalanche.qc.ca*) has worked since 1999 to raise awareness and prevent these types of disasters, which have killed some 30 people in Québec since 1970. Gaspésie accounts for 40% of these accidents, including two deaths in 2000. Before setting out, you should look up the current risk of avalanche for the day you visit Parc national de la Gaspésie.

nine months of the year, and the mean temperature year-round is –3.6°C. As for wind, the most violent gusts ever measured on Mont Logan reached 180km/h. This cold climate and large snowfall explains the lateness of the spring flood on the park's rivers: Rivière Sainte-Anne reaches its highest level in June.

Natural Landscapes

As you scale the mountains of Parc national de la Gaspésie, you pass from one vegetation area to another. Within a few short hours of walking, the contrast is stark, separating dense fir and birch forest in the valley from bare, windswept crags.

■ The Montane Belt

This zone includes the lower altitudes of the park, between 60m and 900m above sea level. The montane belt is mainly cover by fir and white birch, with fir and yellow birch in lower areas.

Besides yellow and white birch, white spruce and other coniferous trees such as balsam fir and cedar also grow here.

■ The Subalpine Belt

This zone, between 900m and 1,100m in altitude, is dominated by conifers. The forest is less dense than in the montane belt, and small clearings appear. The main species in the subalpine stage are white spruce, black spruce, and balsam fir.

■ The Alpine Belt

The realm of treeless barrens and lofty peaks above 1,100m is the alpine belt. The vegetation here is similar to the Arctic tundra, albeit created by high altitude rather than high latitude. The flora is similar to the tundra: stunted or "krummholz" conifers and lichens. A veritable enclave of arctic tundra in southern Québec, this alpine zone occupies over 32km^2.

■ Old-Growth Forest

Designated an "exceptional forest ecosystem," some twenty pockets of old-growth forest have been identified in the park. These are virgin forests unspoiled by natural catastrophes (epidemics, fires, etc.) and by human activity. The forest is dominated by very old trees, with some specimens of white spruce up to 260 years old and some balsam firs up to 150 years old. These ancient trees are flanked by their predecessors lying on the ground, in various states of decomposition; young saplings grow in the small clearings torn open by their fall.

An essential pillar of the boreal forest's biodiversity, these pockets of old-growth forest allow numerous species of plants and animals to flourish. Certain animals such as caribou, rodents, amphibians, and birds (Black-Backed Woodpeckers, Brown Creepers, and Boreal Chickadees) are particularly fond of old-growth forest.

■ The Mont Albert Tundra

The high altitude provides the conditions necessary for the development of the tundra, but this is not the only factor affecting the natural environment of Mont Albert. This mountain is largely made up of serpentine, a rock rarely found on the surface of the earth; this rock is quite toxic for several plant species, while others only grow on serpentine, such as sea thrift and serpentine stitchwort.

Wildlife Watching

The high peaks and deep valleys of Parc national de la Gaspésie allow visitors to observe a surprising number of animal species in a small area. Several species that cannot be found within a hundred kilometres of one another elsewhere in Québec can be seen together within the park. This is the case for Québec's three species of deer: the white-tailed deer, the moose (or elk), and the woodland caribou.

Mammals

■ White-Tailed Deer

At the foot of the mountains, the valleys of Rivière Sainte-Anne and its tributaries host a small population of white-tailed deer. These deer face much more challenging conditions in Gaspésie than elsewhere in southern Québec: the harsh winters and heavy snowfall impede the animals' movements and cause many deaths.

Films on Moose Behaviour

Naturalist Gisèle Benoit has produced two excellent films on the behaviour of moose in Gaspésie. The prizewinning documentaries *En compagnie des orignaux* and *L'Esprit de l'orignal* tell of her 12 years of patient observation of this huge mammal. Both science and storytelling, these documentaries bear witness to the unusual rapport between the naturalist and the moose, and to a profound respect for the animal world.

■ Moose

Better adapted to the rigours of its life than its smaller cousin the white-tailed deer, the moose (known in Europe as the elk) is the largest member of the deer family in Québec. Moose are easy to spot in Parc national de la Gaspésie, with densities up to 20 head per 10km². The white birch and fir forest in parts of the montane zone, the young saplings, and the absence of hunting all serve to create an ideal environment for moose, much to the pleasure of visitors eager to spot this remarkable creature.

■ Woodland Caribou

The name "caribou" is thought to come from the Mi'kmaq word for "scratcher," referring to this animal's habit of finding food by scratching the dirt with its forefeet. The woodland caribou of Parc national de la Gaspésie are the last wild herd south of the St. Lawrence. This "relic herd" represents a species that once ranged throughout eastern North America, but has disappeared completely from the Maritimes, Great Lakes region, and New England since the end of the 19th century. Even in Gaspésie, the current herd is only a quarter of what it was fifty years ago.

Currently, about 80% (542km²) of the herd's population is within Parc national de la Gaspésie. Since this population has evolved separated from the herds in northern Québec, it is genetically distinct.

Parc national de la Gaspésie - Wildlife Watching - Mammals

Meeting Caribou

The use of the park by hikers has been observed to increase the movements of caribou. This has led to certain restrictions being placed on trails and summits. If you meet a caribou while hiking, be discreet; do not leave the path, stay silent, and do not move. Despite the best conservation efforts, the caribou's situation in Parc national de la Gaspésie remains precarious. In 2001, the park's caribou were designated "endangered" by the Committee on the Status of Endangered Wildlife in Canada (COSEWIC). This designation could be removed if the 2002-2012 recovery plan proves successful.

According to telemetry studies carried out between 1998 and 2001, the park's caribou are divided into three subgroups inhabiting Mont Logan, Mont Albert, and the McGerrigle Mountains respectively. They represent some 200 head in total (2006), and their survival is far from guaranteed. The recovery of the Gaspésie caribou herd is in the hands of a committee bringing together all involved government wildlife and ecology officers.

Among the factors impacting the caribou population is predation. Black bears and coyotes take advantage of the vulnerability of young caribou during the first six months of life. We now know that the alteration of caribou habitat near the park has had a significant impact. Logging has replaced mature forests favourable to caribou with young stands that promote increased bear and coyote populations.

A recovery program for the park's caribou population was implemented at the beginning of the 1990s. A second recovery program (2002-2012) aims to ensure that fawns reach 17% of the population every year, thereby providing the herd with the best chance of survival.

■ **Coyotes**

Unlike the moose or caribou, the coyote is a newcomer to Parc national de la Gaspésie. This prowler, more commonly associated with the Midwestern plains, did not arrive in Québec until 1944, attracted by agriculture, forestry and the extermination of the wolf in southern Québec. The coyote first appeared in Sainte-Anne-des-Monts in 1972.

The versatile coyote is one of the few animal species to have expanded its range over the last century. However, the boreal forest in Parc national de la Gaspésie is not ideal for it. The coyote is known to attack caribou fawns, but it prefers white-tailed deer, hares, beavers, groundhogs, and berries.

■ **Black Bear**

With its range extending from Florida to Alaska, it is not surprising to find the black bear in Parc national de la Gaspésie. Though it fasts for several months during its hibernation, when up and about it is an omnivore and one of Québec's greatest meat eaters. It can also eat plants, fruits, and ants, besides actively preying on fawns.

Birds

Since 1920, ornithologists have observed 158 species of birds in Parc national de la Gaspésie.

According to the Committee on the Status of Endangered Wildlife in Canada (COSEWIC), 5 of these 158 species are on the list of "threatened or vulnerable species or species likely to be so designated." Of these, the Bicknell's Thrush, the Golden Eagle, and the Harlequin Duck are the most likely to be spotted during a visit to the park.

■ **Alpine Breeders**

Three breeding species frequent the park's alpine environment. The Horned Lark favours bare summits, and the tundra-dwelling American Pipit and Common Redpoll have also been spotted in the park.

Fish

Atlantic salmon and brook trout are the main species in the rivers and lakes of Parc national de la Gaspésie. However, other species make their home here, such as lake trout, Arctic char, ninespine and brook sticklebacks, and eels.

Species in Peril		
Species	**Problem**	**Range**
Harlequin Duck	Small population (under 1,500) in eastern North America due to water pollution	Certain Gaspésie rivers, in particular Rivière Sainte-Anne
Bald Eagle	Only 26 pairs known in Québec; human use of their nesting sites	Riverbanks, lakes, and rivers
Bicknell's Thrush	Fragmentation and loss of habitat; atmospheric pollution	Montane forest between 450m and 915m
Golden Eagle	Population estimated at 60 pairs in Québec	Sparse mountain areas and inaccessible cliffs
Peregrine Falcon	Capture, hunting, nest disturbance	Mountains and cliffs

Discovery and Visitors Centre

Even if you've spent hours in the car and are longing to stretch your legs on the trails in the park, a few minutes in the modern Discovery and Visitors Centre is essential. Located near Gîte du Mont-Albert, this centre offers valuable information on the natural environment you have just entered. The permanent exhibit called *A Sea of Mountains in the Heart of the Gaspé Peninsula* details the various corners of Parc national de la Gaspésie and its natural and historic heritage. The self-guided visit takes less than an hour.

■ Atlantic Salmon

Rivière Sainte-Anne, where the first recorded fishing expedition dates to 1870, is one of the Gaspé Peninsula's 18 salmon runs. Some 20 salmon pools are accessible to anglers.

Salmon return to their native river to reproduce, recognizing it by a mysterious "smell." They climb Rivière Sainte-Anne at the beginning of summer, ending at the falls near Gîte du Mont-Albert. Breeding takes place in autumn. Some salmon then return to the sea, while others spend the winter in the river and return to the sea with the spring flood.

■ Other Species

Among the other species in Parc national de la Gaspésie, lake trout have been introduced to Lac Thibault, while lake trout and Arctic char can be found in several lakes. Like the caribou, the Arctic char is considered a relic species, trapped 8,000 years ago in Gaspésie's lakes when the last glacier melted.

Where to Observe Wildlife

Many visitors to Parc national de la Gaspésie come across moose; they can be seen at Lac Paul feeding on aquatic plants in the summer, and on Mont Ernest-Laforce in the

Parc national de la Gaspésie - Wildlife Watching - Where to Observe Wildlife summer and the autumn. White-tailed deer are more difficult to find because of their low population; they frequent the low-altitude forests in the Sainte-Anne river valley. As for caribou, they are easier to spot as they frequent sparse subalpine forests and treeless summits. They are most often seen on Mont Jacques-Cartier.

Observing Popular Wildlife Species in Parc National de la Gaspésie			
Species	**Location**	**Period**	**Chance of Observing**
Gaspésie woodland caribou	Mont Jacques-Cartier	June 24 to September 30	Excellent
Gaspésie woodland caribou	Mont Albert	Mid-June to September 30	Good
Moose	Mont Ernest-Laforce	Mid-May to early November	Excellent
Moose	Lac Paul	Mid-June to early August	Good
Moose	Belvédère Le Brûlé	Mid-May to early November	Excellent
Golden Eagle	Mont Ernest-Laforce	Mid-May to mid-August	Excellent
Golden Eagle	Mont Olivine	Mid-August to early November	Good
Harlequin Duck	Rivière Sainte-Anne	Late April to early June	Excellent

Salmon breed in a shallow section of Rivière Sainte-Anne, easily accessible from Gîte du Mont-Albert. The excellent viewing conditions allow a rare glimpse at the fascinating reproductive behaviour of salmon. The area in question is beside the path between the La Rivière campground and the Chute Sainte-Anne waterfall.

Spruce Grouse	Parc national de la Gaspésie	Year-round	Good
Bicknell's Thrush	Mont Jacques-Cartier	June 24 to mid-July	Very good
Bicknell's Thrush	Mines Madeleine	June 24 to mid-July	Excellent
Atlantic salmon	Rivière Sainte-Anne (sanctuary)	Mid-October to mid-November	Excellent
Atlantic salmon	Rivière Sainte-Anne (Grande Fosse lookout)	Late June to late September	Good
Brook trout	Lac aux Américains	Mid-May to early November	Excellent
Brook trout	Mont Jacques-Cartier (Lac à René)	June 24 to September 30	Excellent

Overview of Activities

Summer and winter alike, Parc national de la Gaspésie welcomes outdoor lovers with its vast horizons, accessible like few others in Québec. Whether you prefer to hike foot or snowshoes or explore a river with a paddle or a fishing rod in hand, there are many paths into the Gaspesian wilderness.

The Discovery and Visitors Centre provides a helpful relief model, allowing visitors to familiarize themselves with the park's trails and giving them a better idea of the effort each requires. The park's staff is available to answer any questions and provide information. Numerous reference books and field guides are also available.

The centre also includes a convenience store, a Boutique Nature, an outdoor equipment rental service, (hot!) showers, a laundry room, and a luggage check.

Self-Guided Tour

The park offers several discovery trails with interpretive panels. These routes are great ways to discover the varied natural habitats and their importance to animal species. You can find these trails on the park map.

Discovery Tour with a Park Warden

There are endless ways to discover the treasures of Parc national de la Gaspésie.

Discovery tours led by park wardens open doors to unexpected discoveries—and these are many.

This land of contrasts and precious natural treasures offers several guided tours of its wonders. Depending on your physical condition and your curiosity, you can choose between exploring rare phenomena unique to the park, the peculiar geological origin of Mont Albert, or Mont Jacques-Cartier, Québec's second-highest mountain at 1,270m. The climate and plant life of this tundra-like summit make it a universe unto itself that resembles Québec's Far North.

A less demanding activity explores the ecosystem of the king of the park, the moose. With a little luck, will, and silence, you may come face to face with the world's largest cervid. Even more relaxing is a canoe trip to discover the marvels of long, narrow Lac Cascapédia, hemmed in on all sides with 800m-high mountains.

Other Discovery Activities

Other discovery activities in Parc national de la Gaspésie give you the chance to discover the park's geology, its history, or one of its most famous and most threatened inhabitants, the caribou. Visitors of all ages can also learn about other aspects of the land through a play for all ages about the inhabitants of the tundra and a story-telling activity on how the first explorers adapted to the rigours of the elements.

Summer Activities

In the mountains or on the river, on foot or in a canoe, everyone can discover the park's summertime delights. But although summer is by far the most comfortable time to visit, beware of foul weather! Strong winds and even the occasional unseasonable snowstorm can catch you by surprise at high altitudes.

■ Hiking

Whether your tastes run to a 1.5km stroll or a multi-day trek of 110km, the seemingly endless universe of mountains in Parc national de la Gaspésie has a trail for you. A shuttle service offers transportation to various important sites in the park, in particular the departure point for the Mont Jacques-Cartier trail.

■ One-Day Hikes

The hikes listed below are for one-day hikes, no longer than 17.2km or 8h of walking. The shorter hikes lead to natural heritage sites, while the others lead to various peaks throughout the park. All trails are open from June 24 to September 30, with certain trails open from May through November. The distances listed are for a round trip or complete loop, depending on the trail.

··· Trails leaving from the Discovery and Visitors Centre

Chute Sainte-Anne

A good introduction to the park, especially for those who don't have much time, this is the shortest trail in the park at barely 1.6km or a half-hour of walking. Near Route 299, this easy trail runs along Rivière Sainte-Anne. The main attraction, the view of Chute Sainte-Anne waterfall, also reveals the escarpments of Mont Albert. Ten-metre-high Chute Sainte-Anne is most impressive in June when the snows melt, but can also swell suddenly later in the summer after a large rainstorm.

La Lucarne

Another short and easy hike, La Lucarne is a 1.9km loop taking about an hour. The trail leads to La Lucarne viewpoint, high enough to provide a 360° panorama.

La Saillie

A slightly more challenging trail with a mild slope, this 3.2km (about 1h30) intermediate-level trail runs west from Gîte du Mont-Albert and Rivière Sainte-Anne. It includes the departure point for the Mont Albert trail, but stops 150m up at the La Saillie lookout. The view of Gîte du Mont-Albert and the Rivière Sainte-Anne valley is magnificent, as is the dense boreal forest on either side of the trail.

Chute du Diable

The Chute du Diable trail is more of an effort, with 7km of intermediate-level hiking. The trail rises 200m and requires about 3h to walk. The trail approaches but does not reach the Chute du Diable waterfall, and you can only see its top half; the waterfall is part of Ruisseau du Diable, a stream that drains the eastern face of Mont Albert into Rivière Sainte-Anne.

La Serpentine

The first part of this trail, ranked difficult, follows the Chute du Diable trail. If you're hiking the Chute du Diable trail and you find you're making good time, you can choose to continue a little further to the La Serpentine shelter. After Chute du Diable, you walk beside part of Lac du Diable at an altitude where trees are already becoming sparse. Above the lake, you walk along Ruisseau du Diable until the La Serpentine shelter. The whole trail is 12.5km long and rises 300m. It takes about 4h to walk the trail starting from the Discovery and Visitors Centre.

Mont Albert

To reach the 1,070m-high north peak of Mont Albert (the south peak is higher at 1,154m but there is no trail), you have a choice of trails. The shorter of the two, passing by the La Saillie lookout, is an 11.4km (5h) loop. Rising 870m, it is ranked difficult.

The Les Rabougris shelter is the gateway to the vast (13km^2) mountaintop plateau, where caribou can be spotted browsing on the alpine flora. Don't forget your binoculars! A little further on, the Le Versant observation deck offers an impressive view of Vallée du Diable. Turn back here if you only want to scale the mountain, not go around it.

Tour du Mont Albert

The other way to take in the splendour of Mont Albert is to take the whole day (6-8h) to go all the way around it. While this trail leads to the same summit as the previous trail, it is a loop, allowing you to enjoy the hike without retracing your steps. Accordingly, this trail is longer (17.2km) and more challenging (ranked very difficult). After reaching the Le Versant observation deck, you will enter the gigantic glacial valley of Ruisseau du Diable. You will then arrive at the La Serpentine shelter before following Rivière Sainte-Anne the rest of the way.

This trail's great length makes a number of stops—the La Saillie and Le Versant observation decks, the Chutes du Diable and Chute Sainte-Anne waterfalls, the Les Rabougris and La Serpentine shelters, and of course the great 13km^2 plateau at the northern peak of Mont Albert, with its grazing caribou. A challenge, to be sure—but what a payoff!

··· *Trails leaving from the McGerrigles sector*

Lac aux Américains

Rightly considered one of the most beautiful glacial cirques in Québec, the Lac aux Américains area can be reached by an easy path, barely 2.6km long and without any significant altitude gain. The lake has two giant neighbours, Mont Joseph-Fortin (1,080m) to the south and Mont Xalibu (1,140m) to the north, and is a stopping point on the way up Mont Xalibu. Your walk Lac aux Américains will take about 1h30.

Mont Ernest-Laforce

This 4.5km loop is an inter-mediate-level challenge (a 150m altitude gain, reaching an altitude of 820m), since you go up most of the mountain by car before reaching the parking lot. In any case, the panoramas are incredible, taking in the Mont Albert plateau, the McGerrigle range, and Vallée du Diable. The 2h hike leads through a regenerating forest filled with easily observed animals.

Mont Jacques-Cartier

At 1,270m, Mont Jacques-Cartier is the ultimate Gaspésie mountain experience. In all of Québec, only remote Mont D'Iberville in the far northern Torngat range is higher. On a clear day, from the summit you can see the Chic-Chocs, the plateau of Mont Albert, the St. Lawrence, and sometimes even the river's north shore. But above all, this is the place to see caribou, grazing on the vast expanse of alpine tundra.

This rocky trail, rated difficult, is 8.2km long with a 450m altitude gain, and takes 4-5h of walking. An additional 1km loop near the summit (Le Caribou trail) leads to the majestic Vallée du Cor, where there are excellent chances of seeing caribou.

To protect the caribou, this trail is subject to the park's strictest regulations. The trail is open only from 10am to 4pm (you must leave the summit by 2:30pm to reach the end on time) from June 24 to September 30 inclusively. A shuttle takes visitors from the Mont Jacques-Cartier campground to the trail-head every half-hour from 10am to noon, and returns starting at 2:15pm. A bus also runs between the trailhead and the Discovery and Visitors Centre morning and evening. Information on the caribou is presented at the

Mont Xalibu

After following the Lac aux Américains trail, this difficult trail stretches along a narrow path through dense forest, and then continues along its last third through the alpine tundra. Above the tree line, the view is extraordinary, with Lac aux Américains dwindling in the distance. Allow 5-6h for this 10.7km trail, which reaches an altitude of 1,140m with a gain of 540m.

Mont Joseph-Fortin and Mont Richardson

Together with Mont Xalibu, Mont Joseph-Fortin (1,080m) hems in the Lac aux Américains glacial cirque. Its summit can be reached by this 10km (4-5h) trail, rated difficult for its altitude gain of 480m. The trail to the summit of Mont Richardson is harder (rated very difficult), with an altitude gain of 600m over 16km; you will need 6h to scale the 1,180m mountain and return.

The trail follows an old prospectors' road. A short 0.7km detour leads to the La Falaise observation deck, with a view of the Ruisseau du Portage valley below with Mont Ernest-Laforce in the background. Back on the trail, you will come to a fork in the road, with the left-hand path leading to Mont Joseph-Fortin and the right-hand path leading to Mont Richardson. At the summit of Mont Joseph-Fortin, the trail becomes a loop leading to the Le Surplomb observation deck, with a vertiginous view of Lac aux Américains some 400 metres below.

Mont Richardson, for its part, delights the eye with its wild, unspoiled beauty. Sharper than the characteristic rounded peaks of the region, this mountain has no shelters, observation decks, or anything else besides the vast alpine tundra of the McGerrigles.

··· Trails leaving from the Lac-Cascapédia campground

Pic du Brûlé and Mont Ernest-Médard

The 13.2km loop leading to the 790m-tall Pic du Brûlé provides a 5h hike rated as difficult due to its 330m altitude gain. The L'Éboulis observation deck surveys the horizon and offers a bird's-eye view of the foothills.

··· *Trails leaving from Ruisseau Isabelle or the Discovery and Visitors Centre*

Mont Olivine

Mont Olivine's two trails mean that you can choose not to double back; if this is what you prefer, park your car at the other end of the trail from where you start. The 8km trail rises 450m, and you can scale the mountain in about 4h. The 670m summit provides a spectacular view of Mont Albert.

■ Long-Distance Hiking

La Grande Traversée

The long-distance hiking network of Parc national de la Gaspésie, created in 1992, includes 110km of trails connecting 14 eight-person shelters, between 6.6km and 19km apart, and numerous campsites. It is essential to make reservations for shelters and campsites with park authorities.

Also called La Grande Traversée (the great crossing), this network is part of the Québec segment of the International Appalachian Trail. You can spend two days hiking a small section, or cross the entire park in 10 days. The route described here crosses the whole park from west to east, ending at the Mont-Jacques-Cartier campground. You can also begin the trail even further west along the International Appalachian Trail in the Réserve faunique de Matane, and continue eastward to Cap Gaspé in Forillon National Park.

La Grande Traversée crosses the home of the moose and caribou. Kilometre-high summits, alpine tundra, wetlands, narrow valleys, near-eternal snows, mountainside crests, and Gaspésie's king of mountains, Mont Jacques-Cartier, are just some of the treasures it has in store.

From west to east, this trail crosses the park, in turn passing Mont Logan at the western tip, the Lac Cascapédia service area, the centre of the park, Mont Albert, and the Discovery and Visitors Centre. To the east, Mont Jacques-Cartier, Québec's second-highest mountain, is the last summit of the hike.

For your convenience, the park offers transportation from the Cascapédia and Mont-Albert service areas to certain shelters in the back country. This allows you to explore the far reaches of your park and then return to your car.

■ Canoeing, Canoe-Camping and Kayaking

Lac Cascapédia, 4.5km long, is the largest and most accessible lake in Parc national de la Gaspésie. You can visit it by kayak or canoe, which are available for rent at Lac-Cascapédia campground. Another campground, halfway along the lake, allows a third option, canoe-camping for exploring Lac Cascapédia's enchanting beauty. Get up early on a misty morning or set off on a hot afternoon to spot the moose that live along the lakeshore.

■ Stream and Lake Fishing

Parc national de la Gaspésie offers a number of opportunities to fish for trout. Visitors interested in fishing must first obtain a park permit, which we recommend reserving in advance.

The park's lakes and watercourses can be fished from a canoe, which you can rent, or from a wild riverbank. If you are tempted by the idea of a real fishing holiday over several days, inquire about the fishing packages including cabin rental.

■ Salmon Fishing

The cool waters draining from the Chic-Chocs are an ideal salmon habitat. Salmon fishing is offered in the upper part of Rivière Sainte-Anne between the northern boundary of the park and Chute Sainte-Anne near Gîte du Mont-Albert.

A private company offers services for anglers along the whole river. These include packages for learning to fly-fish for salmon, including the services of a guide. Large salmon must be released throughout the entire fishing season, from June 15 to September 30.

Packages with a guide and canoe include room and board in the Petit-Sault cabins, about 12km downriver from Gîte du Mont-Albert.

■ Mountain Biking

The park offers three mountain biking trails, around Lac Cascapédia. The first, ranked easy, runs 13km round trip between Lac Paul and the

Cross-Country Ski Trails			
Trails	**Length**	**Time**	**Difficulty**
Du Camping	4.5km	1h (round trip)	Easy
Des Fourches	4.5km	1h30 (loop)	Easy
Du Ruisseau-du-Portage	10km	3h (loop)	Difficult
Du Lac-aux-Américains	16km	5h (round trip)	Difficult

Huard hut. The second, ranked intermediate, is 40km long and extends from Lac Cascapédia to the Refuge du Huard hut. Finally, an expert-level trail runs from the Huard hut to Mont Logan (44km round trip). You can reserve accommodations at the Huard hut in advance.

Winter Activities

With 7m of powder snow transforming it into a wild fairyland every winter, Parc national de la Gaspésie is the delight of winter sport buffs. Strap on your snowshoes or skis, pit the strength of your legs against some of the highest mountains in Québec,

and find out what the park has to offer in the winter.

■ Cross-Country Skiing

Parc national de la Gaspésie has a network of 24km of mechanically groomed cross-country ski trails, all starting from the Discovery and Visitors Centre.

■ Long-Distance Skiing

This is the ultimate way to explore the deep, snow-covered forests and bare, windy peaks of Parc national de la Gaspésie. You must be prepared to confront highly variable weather conditions ranging from beautiful sunny days at −30°C to blizzards that drop 40cm of snow overnight. For this reason, we recommend you only attempt these excursions with at least two other people.

About 190km of marked trails are available here, with 14 shelters where you can warm up and rest for the next day. Sleeping in its huts at night and gliding through its breathtaking landscapes by day, you'll truly live and feel the park.

The routes listed below are examples of excursions you can make on the cross-country ski trails. For an additional fee, you can have your baggage transported by snowmobile.

McGerrigle Mountains

This 31km loop is a 3-day excursion from the Discovery and Visitors Centre. After 8km through the forest, you'll reach the Roselin hut beside Lac aux Américains. Next, a trail along the foot of the ridge takes you 11km to the Mines Madeleine hut. On the third day, you'll ski the last 12km to return to the Discovery and Visitors Centre. This loop is rated easy.

La Paruline and Le Pluvier

Ideal for your first experience with long-distance skiing, this loop runs 34km (three days and two nights) through the Lac Cascapédia area. Access is via a parking lot located 4km south of the park entrance, on Route 299. First, an uphill ski of 9.5km takes you to the Paruline hut. Over the next two days, you continue to the Pluvier hut on Lac Cascapédia, before returning to the La Boussole parking lot along a very welcome downward slope.

Cascapédia

This 57km trail circles Lac Cascapédia, with stops at the Pluvier (first and fourth nights), Huard, and Mésange huts. The first day has a long trek up a deceptively flat-looking but uphill stretch. Afterwards, the hike continues along narrower trails deep in the forest, with viewpoints overlooking a scattering of lakes.

Although this trail is considered intermediate in difficulty, the days are uneven, with some being hard and others easy— the second day is the longest at 20km, while the third day is only 6km. You will need five days to complete the circuit.

Snowshoe Trails

Trail	Departure Point	Difficulty	Length	Altitude Gain	Time	Type
Chute Sainte-Anne	Discovery and Visitors Centre	Easy	1.6km	Low	0h30	Round trip
La Lucarne	Discovery and Visitors Centre	Easy	1.9km	Low	0h45	Loop
La Saillie	Discovery and Visitors Centre	Intermediate	3.2km	150m	1h30	Round trip
Chute du Diable	Discovery and Visitors Centre	Intermediate	9km	200m	3h	Round trip
La Serpentine	Ruisseau Isabelle	Intermediate	10km	Low	3h	Round trip
La Serpentine	Discovery and Visitors Centre	Difficult	12.2km	300m	5h	Round trip
Mont Olivine	Ruisseau Isabelle	Intermediate	8km	400m	4h	Round trip
Mont Olivine	Discovery and Visitors Centre	Difficult	12km	450m	6h	Round trip

Lac aux Américains	Discovery and Visitors Centre	Difficult	16km	350m	5h	Round trip
Champ-de-Mars	Réserve faunique Chic-Chocs	Intermediate	5.2km	330m	2h30	Round trip
Mont Hog's Back	Réserve faunique Chic-Chocs	Difficult	6km	350m	3h30	Round trip

Logan

This round-trip trail starts outside the park, at the Relais Chic-Chocs in the village of Saint-Octave-de-l'Avenir. To get to the village, leave Route 132 (which runs along the St. Lawrence) at Cap-Chat, and head inland. Varying between 8km and 22km per day, this trail has more hard days than easy ones. There are stops at the Huard, Carouge, Chouette, and Nyctale huts, as well as the summit of fabled Mont Logan (1,128m). The 70km round trip takes five days to complete.

■ Snowshoes

For the most part, the snowshoe trails in Parc national de la Gaspésie follow the summer hiking trails; accordingly, for more details on what you'll see during your excursion, please see the hiking section (p. 81).

Note that only Route 299 is ploughed in winter, so all trails start along this highway.

Besides the summer trails, snowshoe trails also ascend Mont Hog's Back and Mont Champ-de-Mars, both about 800m high. These are situated outside Parc national de la Gaspésie, in Réserve faunique des Chic-Chocs to the south, but are still managed by Sépaq.

■ Sliding Sports

Thrill-seekers who never get enough are in their glory here, since the park's abundant dry,

Parc national de la Gaspésie - Overview of Activities - Winter Activities

Sliding Sports				
Trail	**Departure Point**	**Length**	**Altitude Gain**	**Time**
Champ-de-Mars	Réserve faunique des Chic-Chocs	5.2km	330m	2h30
Mont Blanche-Lamontagne	Réserve faunique des Chic-Chocs	16km	650m	6h
Mont Hog's Back	Réserve faunique des Chic-Chocs	6km	350m	3h30
Mur des Patrouilleurs	Ruisseau Isabelle parking lot	10km	650m	4h
La Grande Cuve	Ruisseau Isabelle parking lot	16.2km	300m	5h30

powdery snow, so cruelly lacking elsewhere in Québec, is perfect for sliding sports such as telemark, snowboarding, and alpine touring. There are no ski lodges or ski lifts here, and correspondingly fewer skiers; all the better to enjoy the beauty of the unspoiled landscapes, and win the delicious satisfaction of making your own mark as you plunge down the slopes.

Parc national de la Gaspésie and its environs have five trails leading to wilderness skiing locations, sometimes after hikes of several hours, in the Mont Albert area and Réserve faunique des Chic-Chocs. These trails are considered very difficult, especially the loop leading to Mont Blanche-Lamontagne. In all cases, we advise using climbing skins (formerly sealskins) for a quicker and easier climb. It is also essential to be cautious and watch out for the weather at the summits, which often suffer high winds, blizzards, and storms.

You must also be aware of the risk of avalanche, which is much higher in wilderness skiing. Park authorities do not allow wilderness skiing except for those who are familiar with avalanches, are able to evaluate the stability of the snow when they arrive, have emergency equipment, and are in groups of three or more people.

Practical Information

Lodging

■ Primitive Camping

Several primitive campgrounds are accessible on foot or by canoe. They offer a unique experience amid the grand natural spaces of the park. These campgrounds have wooden platforms to pitch your tent on and pit toilets nearby. Fires are forbidden.

■ Serviced Camping

The park's serviced campgrounds, with 212 campsites, occupy four central, accessible locations in the park: Mont Albert, Mont Jacques-Cartier, Lac Cascapédia, and Rivière Sainte-Anne. These are excellent base camps for resting between hikes. These campgrounds are accessible by car and offer showers, toilets, electricity, and fireplaces.

■ Winter Camping

A treat for people who don't suffer from the cold, winter camping is available at the Mont Albert campground only. The washroom facility with washbasin and shower is open year-round, but campfires are prohibited even in winter.

■ Huts

More comfortable than a tent but less elaborate than a cabin, staying in a hut is a special experience "off the grid" and back to nature. The huts are shelters that you reach at the end of a day of walking, skiing, or snowshoeing, and are heated with a wood stove. The park's 16 huts sleep 8 people each, except for the Huard hut, which can host 16.

■ Cabins

Located near Rivière Sainte-Anne, Gîte du Mont-Albert, and Lac Cascapédia, the park's 33 charming and comfortable cabins each offer kitchenettes and beds with mattresses (only the 25 cabins at Gîte du Mont-Albert provide linens). They sleep two to six people each.

■ Gîte du Mont-Albert

Gîte du Mont-Albert, a long white building that blends in perfectly with the mountain atmosphere, is a Gaspesian jewel. The four-star hotel is largely responsible for the reputation enjoyed by Parc national de la Gaspésie abroad.

Since 1950, this inn has occupied an enchanting mountain site between the Chic-Chocs and McGerrigle mountain ranges and earned an extra-ordinary reputation for quality and hospitality. Its 60 rooms (48 at the hotel and 12 at the lodge) all offer a view of Mont Albert. The hotel is surrounded by 25 cabins.

Dining

■ The Gîte du Mont-Albert Dining Room

Like the grand natural spaces that surround it, Gîte du Mont-Albert's dining room is spacious and airy, with high ceilings criss-crossed by exposed beams. Despite its distinguished reputation, enhanced by the chandeliers and meticulous place settings, the 200-person dining room has a warm, relaxed ambiance.

After a bracing day amid the thousand natural treasures of the mountains, the sublime gastronomic experience of Gîte du Mont-Albert is the perfect finishing touch. The chef creates delicious haute cuisine using local products; from smoked salmon to forest mushrooms and caribou, the menu cannot fail to astonish and delight you.

A stop at the bar is the perfect way to begin or end your

evening. Relax with a beer before dinner or a nightcap afterwards, admiring the incredible view of majestic Mont Albert. The fireplace completes the relaxing tableau.

■ Le Piedmont

Located in the Discovery and Visitors Centre and open from June to September, Le Piedmont offers a varied family menu. The decor is charming, especially the vast picture window and its splendid view of Mont Albert.

■ Boxed Lunches

Gîte du Mont-Albert offers a boxed lunch service.

Services

■ Discovery and Visitors Centre

In addition to its permanent exhibit called *A Sea of Mountains in the Heart of the Gaspé Peninsula*, an introduction to the natural heritage of Parc national de la Gaspésie, the Discovery and Visitors Centre is an essential stop for visitors to get the information they need

to organize their park excursion. Reception, information, permits, camper registration, a convenience store, ice and firewood for sale, a gift shop, showers, a laundry, and washrooms are all available to start your trip out right.

The Boutique Nature store sells a range of outdoor equipment and souvenirs, as well as clothes and gifts from the Parcs Québec collection. All profits from Boutique Nature go to conservation in Parc national de la Gaspésie.

The centre is open from May to October and December to March.

■ Mont-Albert Camping Station

This camping station offers the following services: reception and information, permits, camper registration, ice and firewood for sale, and washrooms.

■ Lac-Cascapédia Camping Station

This camping station offers the following services: reception and information, camper registration, a convenience store, firewood for sale, kayak, canoe, and row-boat rentals, and washrooms.

■ Mont-Jacques-Cartier Camping Station

This camping station offers the following services: reception and information, permits, camper registration, a Boutique Nature store, a convenience store, firewood for sale, and shuttle tickets. A themed exhibit on caribou is presented in the campground and along the trail to the top of Mont Jacques-Cartier.

Equipment Rental

The Boutique Nature store in the Discovery and Visitors Centre rents outdoor equipment, offering hiking shoes, walking poles, raincoats, backpacks, sleeping bags, and tents.

In winter, the boutique rents snowshoes, cross-country skiing equipment, ski poles, avalanche beacons, and climbing skins (fastened to the bottom of skis to allow climbing).

Transportation

The park authorities have arranged transportation to the heads of certain trails.

• Shuttle from the Mont-Jacques-Cartier campground to the Mont Jacques-Cartier trailhead.

Runs: from June 24 to September 30

• Bus from the Mont-Albert Discovery and Visitors Centre to Mont Jacques-Cartier.

Runs: from June 24 to September 30

• Transport service for long-distance hikers to various points.

Runs: from June 24 to October 9. Reservations required at least 72h in advance.

• Baggage transportation in winter for long-distance skiers. Reservations required at least 72h in advance.

Nearby

Sainte-Anne-des-Monts

Most visitors reach Parc national de la Gaspésie via the north shore of the peninsula, crossing through the little town of Sainte-Anne-des-Monts before branching off to the park.

This town was built along Rivière Sainte-Anne, amid hills that provide wonderful natural lookouts over the St. Lawrence River. A century ago, in 1915, it suffered a devastating fire. Today, the town offers salmon and trout fishing from the riverbank and dock. A few inns offer all the conveniences as well as fine dining rooms overlooking the sea.

Sainte-Anne-des-Monts is also home to Exploramer *(www. exploramer.org)*, a business whose mission is to showcase the biodiversity of the St. Lawrence River. Aquariums and ponds exhibit the fish species that inhabit the river, while inflatable dinghy excursions show off crab and whelk fishing, scientific research, sea mammals, and other aspects of marine life.

Mont-Saint-Pierre

The highway that runs along the northern coast of the Gaspé Peninsula passes through a succession of tiny villages with improbable, poetic names such as Marsoui, Mont-Louis,

Manche-d'Épée, and Grande-Vallée. Hemmed in between the sea and the mountains of Gaspésie, this route is nothing short of enchanting.

Perched atop its signature 411m cliff tumbling headlong into the St. Lawrence, the village of Mont-Saint-Pierre has something for all open air buffs. There are sea kayak excursions and bicycle and hiking trails, but the main attraction is hanggliding, thanks to the town's cliff. Instructors at École de Vol Libre de Mont-Saint-Pierre help novices take flight.

The Mont-Saint-Pierre campground is a short distance from the village in a wooded area along Rivière Mont-Saint-Pierre. With its 163 campsites, it is an excellent starting point for hiking in the region. A summer road links Mont-Saint-Pierre to the Mont-Jacques-Cartier campground in Parc national de la Gaspésie.

Chic-Chocs Mountain Lodge

At the heart of Réserve faunique de Matane near Parc national de la Gaspésie, the Chic-Chocs Mountain Lodge *(55km south of Cap-Chat, ☎1-800-665-3091 for reservations)* hosts outdoor enthusiasts enjoying alpine touring, snowshoeing, hiking, mountain biking, fishing, or wildlife watching. The intimate lodge has only 18 rooms, as well as a sitting room with fireplace, a sauna, an outdoor whirlpool, and a reputed dining room serving regional products such as fish, duck, caribou, moose, and white-tailed deer. A team of guides is on hand to facilitate outdoor activities and showcase the beautiful nature preserve.

The reception centre and departure point for the shuttle to the lodge (which you cannot reach in your own car) are at Bistro Chez Valmont *(10 Rue Notre-Dame E., Route 132, ☎418-786-1355)*, in Cap-Chat.

Association touristique régionale de la Gaspésie
357 Route de la Mer
Sainte-Flavie, Québec G0J 2L0
☎1-800-463-0323 or 1-877-77J-AIME
www.tourisme-gaspesie.com/en

PARC NATIONAL DE L'ÎLE-BONAVENTURE-ET-DU-ROCHER-PERCÉ

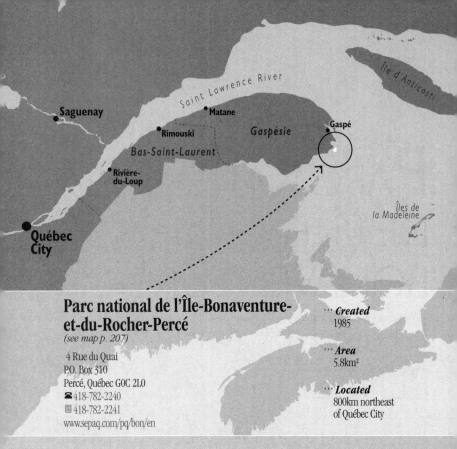

Parc national de l'Île-Bonaventure-et-du-Rocher-Percé

(see map p. 207)

4 Rue du Quai
P.O. Box 310
Percé, Québec G0C 2L0
☎ 418-782-2240
🖷 418-782-2241
www.sepaq.com/pq/bon/en

··· **Created**
1985

··· **Area**
5.8km²

··· **Located**
800km northeast
of Québec City

Our Highlights

- Rocher Percé at sunset, when the last rays turn the rock faces golden.

- The gannets: visitors at the top of the cliffs of Île Bonaventure have the view on the largest and most accessible colony of gannets in the world.

- Le Chafaud: the size and authenticity of this wooden building make it a journey through time to the real lives of cod fishers from the period.

Visiting Time

···*One hour*

If you're here at all, it's probably to see Rocher Percé. Well, feast your eyes! Then go learn more about this world-renowned Gaspésie landmark at La Neigère, which houses the Visitors Centre and the park's Boutique Nature store.

···*A half-day*

With a half-day, you can also visit the Le Chafaud Discovery Centre, where you'll learn about the heyday of the cod fishery, and more about the geology, flora, and fauna of the Gaspé Peninsula, Rocher Percé, and Île Bonaventure.

···*A day or more*

A day or more will give you the full experience. As well as the above-mentioned attractions, you can board one of the private boats that ferry visitors to Île Bonaventure. There, you can travel back in time at Maison Le Boutillier, go birdwatching on a guided tour to the gannet colony, or put on your walking shoes for a hike along one of the island trails. You can also take one of the numerous cruises to see the birds, seals, and whales all around.

Many Quebecers count a "*tour de la Gaspésie*" as one of their most precious vacation memories. Many are those who, every or almost every summer, unhesitatingly spend eight or even twelve hours on the road to (or back to) Rocher Percé or Île Bonaventure with its thousands-strong gannet colony.

Naturally, they also come to pause, gaze out over the gulf, and breathe the fresh sea air. Gaspésie is a land of vast distances, and it would be a shame to spend so long on the road just for a brief stop at Rocher Percé and a few photographs.

Parc national de l'Île-Bonaventure-et-du-Rocher-Percé is in itself worth a stay of several days to properly explore it and get to know the land. Everything is organized to make discovering the park as easy as possible. But before setting out on your trip across the Gaspé, take a few minutes to travel across time.

Some History

Rocher Percé: Who Pierced It?

Measuring 475m long and 85m high, Rocher Percé was formed by limestone sediments accumulating in then-warm seas millions of years ago. Despite its 5-million-tonne bulk, its composition makes it fragile and vulnerable to erosion.

Rocher Percé is estimated to shed 300 tonnes of rock per year, and all indications are that it will one day disappear. You still have a little while to visit, though—it still has a good 20,000 years left!

The Prisoner of Rocher Percé

Once, a young Iroquois chief captured by the Mi'kmaq was condemned to death by exposure on Rocher Percé. Exposed on the rock, he was tormented by young Mi'kmaq women who came to pull his hair and pierce his thighs with fish spines.

But one young woman, Mejiga, was seized with compassion and began to feed him in secret. By and by she fell in love with him and planned to free him and run away with him. But before she could do so, the prisoner's body was found on the beach of Anse du Nord, his throat cut.

Distraught with grief, Mejiga disappeared. They say the Great Spirit took pity on her and changed her into a gull. To this day, she wheels about the rock at night, wailing inconsolably.

This vulnerability to erosion is the origin of the famous 20m hole through Rocher Percé ("pierced rock"). Apparently, though, there were once as many as four holes.

Accounts by European sailors of the 16th and 17th centuries tell of four arches. In 1675, Father Leclercq mentioned three openings in his writings, corroborating on a description by Nicolas Denys, seigneur of Percé, who said in 1672 that there was one hole but two others were forming.

A painting from 1760 (the year of the British conquest) by an aide-de-camp in General Wolfe's army depicts the rock with two arches; the third had apparently collapsed. In 1812, Joseph Bouchette, surveyor general of Lower Canada, also recorded two holes.

Finally, in 1845, one of the remaining arches crumbled, leaving a strange isolated tower and leaving the famous rock with only a single hole. Over the years, the obelisk wore away, losing almost a third of its mass in the 1950s.

Fossils

The fragile nature of the rock, composed of ancient marine sediments, leads us to another aspect: its 150 fossil species, including one known from nowhere else, a trilobite known as the "Percé dalmanite."

Remarkably, there are no fish fossils, indicating that the rock was formed before the appearance of fish more than 400 million years ago.

To trace the origins of the first fish, you need to head southwest to Parc national de Miguasha (see p. 139). Though measuring only 0.8km², the site is world-renowned for its fossils of the Devonian age, known as the age of fish. A natural history museum allows visitors to discover plants and fish trapped in the rock 380 million years ago.

The Island and the Cliffs

Île Bonaventure was likely once attached to Rocher Percé, judging by the limestone that composes its northern section. The cliffs to the north and east are also about 90m high, similar to Rocher Percé. Its crumbling walls have proven a boon to seabirds by creating ledges, crevasses, and small grottoes that they can use as nesting sites.

At its highest point, the island rises to 136m above sea level. However, the southern side, facing Chaleur Bay, is much less steep, reaching only 15m.

The western side, facing the town of Percé, consists of small cliffs interrupted by pebble beaches. The ease of access to this area encouraged human settlement.

As the island has an area of 4km², the interior rises gently. Seen from afar, the island resembles a whale.

Baie des Marigots

In the heyday of the cod fishery, fishermen landed in Baie des Marigots to avoid work. The name of the bay comes from the old French expression "*courir le marigot*," meaning "to loaf." Fishermen came to cook mackerel, have a drink, and nap for a while.

Under the French Regime, the fishermen would then go catch a few cod, returning in the evening complaining of a poor catch. But they would promise that the next day would be better, as it would be risky to "*courir le marigot*" twice in a row.

The Saga of the Cod

The cod fishery was long the centre of life for the people of Gaspésie, whether they had lived there all their lives or were just passing through. One of many food sources used by the Aboriginals, it was a source of wealth for the conquerors and a source of misery for generations of fishermen.

In the 17th century, the Percé region, including Île Bonaventure, was recognized as the most important fishing grounds in the Gulf of St. Lawrence. In season, hundreds of fishing boats converged on the area.

The temporary fishing installations of the French Regime were made permanent after the British conquest. Settlement in the Percé region really took off with the arrival of cod fishing companies from the Channel Islands, such as the Charles Robin Company, the John Le Boutillier Company, and Le Boutillier Brothers.

In 1831, Île Bonaventure had a population of more than 170. Several new arrivals came from Jersey, especially the Aubert, Brochet, and Duval families. The Cody family from Ireland was among the oldest on the island, while others arrived from England and elsewhere in Lower Canada.

Gathering Gannet Eggs

The gannet colonies offered the residents of Île Bonaventure a wild, open-air "henhouse" right on their doorsteps. Before the practice was prohibited, the islanders used to gather gannet eggs routinely. However, as the gannet colony was smaller then, most of the birds nested on the cliff faces, requiring the islanders to scale the cliffs with ropes.

This home-made rock-climbing equipment did not make for a stress-free ascent. Clinging to the rock while being attacked by protective gannets had its dangers. Some egg gatherers lost eyes, while one fell to his death in 1836 when the rope securing him to the cliff gave way.

Since the islanders spent the whole week fishing or cultivating the land, eggs were gathered on Sundays. The egg gatherers would miss Mass, much to the indignation of the parish priest.

A Difficult Separation

Île Bonaventure may be separate from the mainland, but nothing could separate it from the clutches of Le Boutillier Brothers, who kept the fishing families it employed perpetually in debt for fishing equipment. It was also the source of scarce jobs during the hungry winter season, such as barrel-building and spinning wool.

This dependence alarmed the parish priest, who wrote in an 1881 report: *Nearly all the Catholic families are poor. Le Boutillier Brothers pays a considerable sum to keep the school open. Its agent has all school matters in hand. I only hope they do not hire a Protestant teacher.*

The community was so poor that the church never had bells. The islanders did not even have the means to buy their own horses to get around or to work the land.

In 1926, the final closure of Le Boutillier Brothers caused an exodus of island families. The 20th century saw the end of the Channel Islands cod companies, replaced by fishing cooperatives that did not see the promised success. For better or worse, this part of Gaspésie turned to forestry and

The *Gougou*

Since the French Regime, Mi'kmaq legend has told of an ogress called the *Gougou* on Île Bonaventure. The Europeans developed their own version of the tale.

A young Breton fisherman, wanting to find out if the legends were real, stole a Mi'kmaq canoe to row to the island. Noticing it was gone, the owner set out with other Natives to search for his canoe. After a long search, they found the canoe drifting with the young man lying in it unconscious.

After they brought him on board, the Breton fisherman came to and told his story. As he walked through the woods, he was surprised and chased by a terrifying creature, with a huge body like a sea lion's, a wrinkled hag's face, and long pointed teeth. Two evil eyes gleamed, and long yellow hair hung down to its chin.

Chased to the edge of a cliff, the boy decided to leap to his death rather than be devoured. But as he fell, he felt two powerful wings catch him up and lay him gently in the canoe, and that was all he remembered.

The people said that only angels could have been responsible for such a rescue. The *Gougou* was never seen again; some Mi'kmaq later reported seeing its body at the foot of the cliff where the young fisherman had jumped…

farming, and for a certain time, sheep herding became an island specialty.

Tourism and Vacationing

Despite every effort, the population continued to decline until only a handful of people spent the winter on the island in the early 1960s. A few dozen people arrived in the summer, including several Americans who had bought houses for a song.

Slowly but surely, Percé and Île Bonaventure became a major vacation spot. At the beginning of the 20th century, this part of the Gaspé welcomed painters, researchers, naturalists, poets, and other vacationers. On Île Bonaventure, the Maloney inn and some of the islanders hosted visitors.

In the 1950s and 1960s, more and more families, couples, and tour groups came to spend the summer in the area. By winter 1967, the last islanders had deserted Île Bonaventure, leaving it entirely to the summer cottagers. A few fishermen's houses remain to bear witness to the cod fishing years.

The Island Cemetery

In 1857, a certain Georges Aubert gave money and land for the construction of a church and the creation of a cemetery. Monsieur Aubert certainly had a use for a church; he married twice and had eleven children.

The appearance of the cemetery has changed over time. The wooden crosses erected by poor families have disappeared. A few tombstones were put up starting in the 1920s, but the only ones that remain are more recent ones from the 1950s.

To preserve their memory, the national park has installed a large commemorative plaque listing the names and causes of death of 89 people buried in the cemetery.

The Creation of the National Park

In 1971, the government of Québec purchased Île Bonaventure to create a nature preserve. It had already been designated a sanctuary in 1919 by the Migratory Birds Convention between Canada and the United States. This first step aimed to protect the gannet colony.

In 1974, the entire Île Bonaventure and Rocher Percé received the status of nature preserve. In 1985, they became a conservation park called Parc de l'Île-Bonaventure-et-du-Rocher-Percé, indicating the Québec government's will to safeguard and enhance the site and make it available to the public. The park's cultural heritage, consisting of the cemetery and some twenty well-preserved buildings, adds to the park's extraordinary natural riches.

The park sector includes a marine protection area extending 100m off the island's coast, as well as the littoral area around the rock between the high and low tide marks.

In 2003, Parc de l'Île-Bonaventure-et-du-Rocher-Percé became a Québec national park.

Where Did Île Bonaventure Get Its Name?

While it seems fairly clear how Rocher Percé got its name, Île Bonaventure is quite another matter. There are a surprising number of possible explanations, such as the following:

• During a storm, Jacques Cartier had his ships moor in Baie de Percé near an island whose name he did not mention in his logs. This was on July 14, 1534, the feast of St. Bonaventure.

• At the end of the 16th century, a French ship named the *Bonaventure* came to the Gulf of St. Lawrence to "hunt and make oil from the large-tusked beasts known as walruses."

• According to the Commission de toponymie du Québec, a map from the period already lists the island under the name "*Bonne aventure.*" It therefore seems probable that the name was known before 1600 and was used by explorers and fishermen. In his writings, Samuel de Champlain in 1603 mentions "*l'isle de Bonne-adventure.*"

Features of the Park

The sea is a haven of life; in Parc national de l'Île-Bonaventure-et-du-Rocher-Percé, the flora includes 574 species of vascular plants and nearly 200 species of seaweed.

More than 130 species of fish and nearly 225 species of birds are found, including some 60 nesting bird species. The extraordinary setting allows visitors to observe some 20 species of sea mammals.

Tides

Twice a day, the sea rises for about six hours on most coasts, then sinks again. The tides are caused by the gravitational attraction of the Moon and, to a lesser extent, the Sun. Tide tables published by Fisheries and Oceans Canada provide a very precise schedule of tide levels.

At Percé, the mean tidal fall (difference between the

level of high and low tide) is about one metre. This temporary flood affects sea life on the shore and contributes to the extraordinary variety of flora and fauna.

Cold Salt Water

Is the Gulf of St. Lawrence as cold as they say? Actually, it's probably even colder. In summer, the surface layer (0 to 50m) varies from –1°C to 16°C, the mid-layer (50m to 180m) from –1°C to 2°C, and the deep layer (180m to 400m) from 2°C to 6°C.

Can the salt water freeze? Certainly. At Percé as elsewhere in the Gulf, a layer of ice used to form every year. Depending on the severity of the winter, ice bridges could form for ten consecutive winters, then disappear for two to three years. But with climate change and the increased use of icebreakers to clear the seaway, the gulf freezes less often.

Seaweed Everywhere

Slippery, gooey seaweed strikes some people as disgusting, but it is part of our everyday lives. Among other things, it is processed into binding agents for ice cream and cosmetics.

Discovery activities in the national park give visitors the opportunity to taste two species of edible seaweed: sea lettuce and dulse.

The Barachois

Unlike the shores of the St. Lawrence estuary, this region is not favourable to the development of wetlands. However, the Percé region is host to the barachois of the bay of Saint-Georges-de-Malbaie. A barachois is a salt bay closed off by a bar, with only a small inlet. This barachois, which is also fed by rivers, has become a salt marsh.

The barachois is a particularly rich habitat. Several species of fish breed and feed here, and many shorebirds also frequent the area.

Seaweed

The sea and seaweed go hand in hand, like the forest and mountains. Without seaweed, the sea would be practically lifeless. The astonishing variety of seaweed on the Percé coasts is nevertheless little known.

Just beyond the tidal zone, forests of giant kelp form a boundary between the deeps and the shallows. Huge and with rippled edges, the leaves of these seaweeds resemble large lasagna noodles.

The shores are frequently littered with seaweed cast up by storms.

Wildlife Watching

Molluscs

Several species of mollusc can be seen along the shore at low tide by anyone who cares to look.

■ Periwinkle

The periwinkle or winkle, with a hard spiral shell, is a native of Europe. Introduced in the early 19th century, it quickly multiplied, and is now abundant in seaweed stands.

■ Limpet

Colloquially called a *chapeau chinois* ("Chinese hat"), the limpet can be distinguished by its simple conical shell. It adheres to rocks and can be found in tidal pools.

■ Blue Mussel

Blue mussels can be seen in great quantities attached to rocks. During certain periods, these molluscs can accumulate enough toxins to prove deadly to anyone who ingests them.

Crustaceans

Crustaceans possess two pairs of antennae, and a hard shell that is flexible but not extendable. They must therefore moult as they grow; a lobster may shed its shell as many as 25 times before ending up on a plate.

■ American Lobster

Before, lobsters were used as fertilizer or food for peasants; now, a controlled fishery supplies them to the choicest restaurants.

The American lobster, the world's largest crustacean, may vary in colour from blue to orange.

Preferring rocky sea floors, it lives in deep water in winter and moves closer to the coastline in summer. The lobster reaches sexual maturity quite late, at 5 or even 8 years of age, so fishers are required to release small specimens.

The Lobstering Profession

At first glance, catching lobster seems a simple process. In the small hours of the morning, the lobster fisher puts a piece of herring or mackerel in a lobster trap, then lowers it to the bottom. The next morning, the fisher pulls up the traps, or "pots."

Baiting and raising 200 lobster pots every morning is enough work, but lobster fishers need to do much more than that. The pots must be set so as to take account of the currents and depth. And lobsters are not found everywhere—the fisher's sixth sense counts for a lot, an intuition stemming from experience passed down from generation to generation.

The local inhabitants retain their traditional right to fish for lobster in the national park's marine area. The season runs from mid-April to early July, so if you want to eat fresh local lobster, you'll have to vacation early.

■ Rock Crab

Widespread on rocky shores, the rock crab can be recognized by its flattened carapace and short limbs. Crabs are popularly reputed to regrow amputated limbs, which is partly true. A limb can be replaced, but only over a succession of moults.

At low tide, crabs dig into the sand or hide under rocks; little surprise, as the crab is a favourite prey of gulls and striped bass.

■ Hermit Crab

With a soft and therefore vulnerable underbelly, the hermit crab does not always rely on its own shell to protect it; instead, it may take over an abandoned whelk shell. Though it lives on the bottom of the ocean, it is sometimes found on muddy or sandy shores or in tidal pools.

■ Gamarrid

The tiny gamarrid can be found in sea water picked up with a bucket. A colloquial name (sideswimmer) describes it well, since the flattened sides of its carapace force it to move sideways by folding its legs.

Gamarrids live from the tidal zone down to a depth of 30m. When the tide goes out, gamarrids hide under rocks, in tidal pools, or amid seaweed.

■ Barnacle

With its characteristic habit of clinging to rocks, pilings, and boat hulls, the barnacle is sometimes taken for a mollusc, but is a true crustacean. It usually clings onto surfaces that face away from the waves.

Other Sea Creatures

Starfish, sea urchins, and sea cucumbers all have spines anchored in their skeletons. These rarely moving invertebrates live below the low tide mark.

Though beachcombers hardly ever spot them, divers can see these interesting organisms in their seabed homes.

■ Starfish

The Gulf of St. Lawrence hosts about a dozen species of starfish. These harmless-seeming creatures are in fact carnivores, feeding on crustaceans, molluscs, and even the occasional small fish; astonishingly, a starfish can eat up to ten mussels a day. Moreover, it has no natural predators, a rare fact for such a small animal.

Usually living on rocky seafloors, starfish sometimes dig into the sand or hide under seaweed while waiting for the tide to return.

■ Sea Urchin

Shaped like a ball covered in spikes, the sea urchin deserves its name—"urchin" is an old word for hedgehog. Also like hedgehogs, they move around slowly and feed mainly on plants.

But the comparisons end there, as sea urchins are really marine invertebrates. Abundant near kelp stands, they graze sea vegetation using their powerful five-toothed mouth parts, known as "Aristotle's lantern."

Despite the protection of their spines, sea urchins are preyed on by gulls, crabs, and even starfish. Their gonads, in the upper part of their shells, are edible, as is their roe.

■ Sea Cucumber

Crawling slowly over the muddy seabed, sea cucumbers are cylindrical, soft-bodied invertebrates with tentacles around their mouths. When in danger, they can emit dangerous or even deadly poisons to ward off predators. They are fished in the Gulf of St. Lawrence for export to Asian markets.

Fish

The region would be incalculably different without the presence of game fish such as plaice, halibut, redfish, and above all, cod. Nor would Île Bonaventure be home to its teeming seabird colonies without the abundant capelin, mackerel, and herring on which they feed. Fish truly are the base of life in the region.

■ Cod

For centuries, cod was the most abundant species in the Gulf of St. Lawrence. As previously discussed, it is intimately linked to the human history of Percé and the Gaspé coast. It was fished, then prepared for salting and drying, and cod liver oil was once very popular in Québec as a winter tonic.

As cod live in huge shoals and spend the summer in the coastal waters of the gulf, they were the ideal prey for a large-scale fishery. They were fished with lines, basket traps, trawlers, and gill nets. During the 1970s, the quotas authorized by Fisheries and Oceans Canada were routinely exceeded.

By the 1980s, the weight of the catch had plummeted from more than 20kg to between 2kg and 4kg; the large spawners had disappeared. Accordingly, the fishery was closed in 1994 until the cod returned.

However, eight years later, the situation remained unchanged. Causes such as climate change and increased seal populations were variously blamed, and the fishery remains closed.

The food chain that includes the cod is very complex. It preys on such species as herring, capelin, crustaceans, and molluscs, while it is hunted in turn by seals, sharks, and whales.

■ Herring

Herring swim long distances from their wintering grounds to feed in the summer. Certain groups of spawners reproduce along the coastline in spring, while others do so in the summer and autumn.

Herring have long been commercially fished with seines and gillnets, both for their flesh and their roe. After a decline in the 1970s, their population has sprung back.

■ Capelin

Capelin live year-round in the waters of the gulf. They spawn in June and July on sand and fine gravel beaches, an event called the "scull." In a fascinating phenomenon, the capelin arrive on Île Bonaventure when the gannets' eggs are hatching, becoming an important food source for the birds.

Capelin are fished with dip nets, seines, and traps. The species still seems to be abundant and free from overexploitation.

■ Mackerel

Mackerel arrive in the Gulf to spawn in July and August. They then become prey to various predators, including gannets, harbour porpoises, and grey seals.

Fishers catch them with traps or gillnets. However, they remain numerous.

Seals

Seals are often considered a pest by the area's residents, who accuse them of damaging fishing equipment, keeping cod stocks from recovering, and transmitting parasites to the cod. However, for many tourists, seeing these marine mammals is a highlight of their trip.

The grey seal and harbour seal live on the shores of Île Bonaventure from April to November. Both live in the Gulf year-round.

■ Grey Seal

Nicknamed *loup-marin* or "sea wolf" in French, probably because of its growling, this widespread species ranges through the Gulf and the Maritimes, and in fact all the way from Labrador to Massachusetts. It can also be found on the coasts of the British Isles, Norway, and Iceland.

It can be distinguished from other seals by its elongated muzzle and larger size. Adult males (bulls) have a black coat speckled with grey, while females (cows) and young (pups) are grey speckled with black.

From April to June, the adults gather on land for the shedding season. Somewhat less gregarious in the summer, they bask instead on shoals uncovered at low tide. In warmer weather they are sometimes seen swimming offshore, enjoying the cool water.

They can fish even for ground species such as plaice and cod, since they can dive as deep as 200m and stay submerged for nearly 25 minutes! They also feed on mackerel, herring, capelin, and sometimes even seabirds.

Unfortunately for wildlife watchers, grey seals are shyer than harbour seals; basking seals usually flee into the sea as boats approach. They must be observed without disturbing them.

■ Harbour Seal

Like the grey seal, this species is also nicknamed "sea wolf" in French. Besides its shorter muzzle, it can also be recognized by its round head. Adults are grey with black spots and whitish rings.

The harbour seal, also called the common seal, is truly a cosmopolitan species. Besides the Gulf of St. Lawrence, the harbour seal lives on both coasts of North America, including the Atlantic coast as far south of Virginia. It can also be found on the northern coasts of Europe and Asia.

This species frequents shallow waters near bays, islets, or reefs. In summer, it spends much of its time on gravel beaches and rocks uncovered at low tide. When the tide returns, it dives to feed and squabbles with its fellows for still-exposed spots.

From July to September during the mating season, bulls and cows gather in areas called haulouts.

The harbour seal feeds on crabs and shrimp, but also eats a wide variety of fish such as herring and mackerel. It also catches ground fish by diving even deeper than grey seals, as far as 400m! It can also stay submerged for as long as a half-hour. However, its usual dives last about three minutes and reach an average depth of 50m.

Cetaceans

Regular whale-watching cruises leave the park to view whales and dolphins, which like all mammals are warm-blooded and nurse their young.

Some cetacean species have teeth, while others do not. Most toothed cetaceans are relatively small and can be distinguished by their pronounced dorsal fin. Around Percé, they are represented by the Atlantic white-sided dolphin.

The larger whales, over 8m in length, have no teeth, but rather baleen, flexible plates that enable them to strain food out of sea water. Baleen whales in the national park include humpback whales, fin whales, and minke whales. While everyone naturally wants to spot the famous, immense blue whale, it takes luck.

As most whales are social creatures, they are usually spotted in groups, known as pods. As whales frequently travel long distances to feed, whale-watching always has an element of chance.

■ Atlantic White-Sided Dolphin

From mid-July to late August, the white-sided dolphin is a frequent site off Percé. At first glance it may be taken for a harbour porpoise, but it can be distinguished by its pointed, backward-curved dorsal fin and its habit of following whale-watching boats. They can sometimes be spotted with fin whales in a pod of 50 to 500 individuals.

■ Minke Whale

Averaging 8m in length, the minke whale is among the smallest of the rorquals, a family of baleen whales. Regularly seen near Percé, it can be distinguished by its finned, curved back, which stays above the water when it dives while its tail is kept under. Sometimes, it breaches several times in a row, leaping out of the water and falling on its back.

The minke whale is easy to observe, sometimes even approaching anchored boats. Minke whales are usually seen one or two at a time, but they are sometimes spotted in larger groups where krill or small fish congregate.

■ Humpback Whale

Often seen in Percé, the humpback whale sometimes gives whale-watchers an impressive show. Despite its size of up to 14m, the humpback whale is very agile, and can leap out of the water several times before falling on its back. Its diffuse blow, sometimes forming a V-shaped cloud, is usually about 3m high, but can reach 10m when blown straight up.

Stout and with the humped back for which it is named, the humpback whale is also distinguished by its long pectoral fins. Its head is covered by small bumps with hairs, thought to be tactile organs used to detect fish.

Often travelling in groups of several individuals, the humpback whale is frequently accompanied by dolphins sharing in the hunt. Hunting humpbacks sometimes become entangled in fishing nets, not only damaging fishing vessels but sometimes causing the whale to drown.

Protected by an international treaty except in Greenland, the humpback whale population is recovering, but is still considered vulnerable in Canadian waters including Percé.

■ Fin Whale

Reaching lengths of up to 24m, the fin whale is difficult to miss. A common species off the Percé coast, it sometimes ranges close to land.

A surfaced fin whale can blow up to 6m high. They often feed by swimming on their side to swallow a school of capelin or krill. When food is abundant, as many as 100 individuals may be found together. Otherwise, the fin whale stays alone or in groups of two or three.

Fin whale calls are so low-pitched that humans cannot hear them. They can only be detected on a recording with a hydroacoustic amplifier.

This species was hunted until an international moratorium in 1972 spurred by its declining population; it is now considered vulnerable. Only Greenlanders now hunt it, for subsistence.

■ Blue Whale

Blue whales are an occasional visitor to Percé, and number about 200 in the Gulf. When it puts in an appearance, however, it is a memorable one: at 33m long, it is the largest animal of all time, exceeding even the largest dinosaurs. Each day, a blue whale consumes four tonnes of krill.

Its vertical blow can reach 9m in height; when it dives, its huge tail is a spectacular sight. Usually solitary, it sometimes appears with one or two others.

High-seas and coastal whaling nearly drove blue whales to extinction. Now, after 30 years of protection, the population is not growing very quickly but there is hope for a better future. The blue whale is considered vulnerable in Canada.

■ North Atlantic Right Whale

If you see a whale with a double V-shaped blow up to 5m high, it may well be a North Atlantic right whale. The species is distinguished by its lack of a dorsal fin and by its habit of sticking its tail out of the water before diving. It varies in size from 15m to 18m.

The right whale ranges along the coast of North America from Labrador to the Gulf of Mexico. This gentle whale allows boats to approach it, which no doubt contributed to its decline. Once among the most common whales of the coast, it was hunted to excess in the Labrador Sea. Despite a whaling ban in place since 1937, it remains an endangered species. It is very occasionally seen off of Percé.

Birds

Île Bonaventure is home to more than 250,000 seabirds and shorebirds. Nowhere else is such a huge concentration of wild birds observable from so close.

You can see them everywhere perched on the cliffs, clustered on plateaus, or wheeling above the sea. Their calls are a constant sonic backdrop. This unique background music of the wind, sea, and bird calls creates an ambiance combining serenity with frantic action.

Île Bonaventure hosts the world's largest colony of Northern Gannets, with nearly 120,000 individuals. By a happy coincidence, it's also the world's most accessible colony as well! The population of Black-Legged Kittiwakes is also the largest in the Gulf of St. Lawrence.

As the island provides other attractive habitats such as shores, fields, and forests, nearly 200 species of birds are found here. Renowned ornithologist and author Roger Tory Peterson lists Île Bonaventure as one of the 12 best bird watching sites in North America.

■ Why This Profusion?

Why do so many seabirds and shorebirds nest here? First, its distance from the coast prevents disruptions that could harm the nesting process. The cliffs are replete with little ledges and crevasses, creating thousands of good nesting sites. The capes, with their open spaces near the sea, also attract plenty of nesting birds.

Food is also just a wingbeat away. Around the island, schools of capelin, herring, and other small fish arrive constantly throughout the season.

The birds' abundance is also explained by their gregarious lifestyle, which offers protection from predators. When a bird cries out to warn of the presence of a fox or bird of prey, others take up the cry, in a display of cohesion that can frighten predators away.

Life in a colony also offers another crucial advantage—synchronized reproduction. Sexually stimulated by the mating of other pairs, the birds soon start to imitate each other. The females are fertilized sooner, and the chicks are more developed at the end of the season, greatly increasing their chances of survival. The chicks also grow better, because their hatching is synchronized with the arrival of schools of little fish at specific points throughout the season, allowing their parents to feed them their fill.

■ Protected by Law

Once hunted to excess for their feathers and meat, as well as their eggs which were a favourite food of sailors and fishers, seabirds and shorebirds are now protected by law.

Northern Gannet

The raucous cries, elongated body, and tapered bill of the Northern Gannet are distinctive, and with a wingspan of up to 1.8m, the gannet is the largest bird in the park.

Clumsy on the ground, it glides and dives with incredible grace. Gannets fly over a school of fish, wheel, then dive in turn to catch their prey. The disoriented fish are snapped up with lightning speed. Plummeting from 30m with their wings folded, gannets can reach a speed of 100km/h!

A gannet eats about a half-kilo of surface fish each day—herrings, capelin, sand lances, smelt, and even mackerel up to 43cm long. The colony as a whole eats about 40 tonnes of fish a day.

Back on land near its nest, the gannet becomes territorial again. Surprisingly, their nests are quite evenly spaced, with 80cm between them—the striking distance of a good peck to protect their territory.

Watching the birds from close up, visitors can see nesting couples engaging in all kinds of rituals such as grooming and beak fencing. This is a way for them to burn off aggression, easing the stress of colony life.

Eggs are laid when the first schools of herring arrive; they hatch when the capelin arrive. Mackerel is available throughout the summer as the chicks grow and develop their plumage.

Common Murre

With a black back and neck and a white throat and belly, this bird, like the superficially similar but unrelated penguins of the Southern Hemisphere, looks like it is wearing a tuxedo.

Its short wings, on which it reaches speeds of up to 75km/h, also serve as fins as it fishes underwater for capelin, herring, and small cod. Fishermen have often found murres caught in their nets 180m deep.

An adult murre eats its weight (1kg) in fish every week, while a chick does so in two days. The chick leaves the nest at the beginning of August at just three weeks of age, while it still cannot fly. It leaps straight off the cliff, gliding to the sea where it joins the adults and begins to migrate, swimming most of the way. This phenomenon is unique: no other species travels so far while so young, without even being able to fly.

There are an estimated 28,000 pairs on Île Bonaventure, but only about twenty on Rocher Percé.

Black and White

An observer will immediately notice that seabirds are usually not one colour; they are normally pale below and dark above. Their pale bellies make them almost invisible to prey below, while black patches on their backs absorb warmth from the sun and help them to see one another more easily while hunting schools of fish.

Black Guillemot

These solitary birds are not very abundant: about 100 pairs on Île Bonaventure and somewhat fewer on Rocher Percé. The Black Guillemot is almost entirely black; only its feet and the inside of its mouth are red. It can swim underwater up to 50m deep.

When to Watch Wildlife

Species	Access	Periods	Likelihood
Grey seal	Presence depends on tides. Around the island, they can be seen on the rocks on the east side, in the Colonies area, or on the northwest side of Baie des Marigots. Accessible by footpaths. Also boat observation.	June to October	Certain
Harbour seal		June to October	Occasional
Baleen whales and right whale	Abundant krill and small fish attract whales. Visitors can watch and learn about whales during commented boat cruises by park wardens. On the island, whales can be seen from several lookouts accessible on foot, especially Chemin du Roy.	June to October	Occasional
White-sided dolphin		Mid-July to mid-August	Occasional
Northern Gannet	A third of the colony lives on the cliffs while the rest are concentrated on the plateau, easy to reach on foot on the Les Colonies trail.	Late March to late October	Certain
Razorbill	This shorebird nests in colonies on the cliffs. Keep your eyes open as this species is less abundant than others. It can be seen by boat or on foot by Baie des Marigots.	Late March to early August	Certain

Common Murre	Commented cruises easily spot these abundant birds nesting on the cliffs.	Late March to early August	Certain
Black Guillemot	This species is not abundant but never fails to turn up. Look closely and be patient. Can be spotted from a cruise or from the island on foot by Baie des Marigots and Anse Mauger.	March to August	Certain
Atlantic Puffin	Nests in a specific location on the cliffs. Only 40 individuals, difficult to see due to abundance of other birds. Boat only.	Late March to September	Uncertain
Black-Legged Kittiwake	Nests at various spots on the cliffs. Can be seen from a cruise or on foot by Baie des Marigots.	Late March to late August	Certain
Herring Gull and Great Black-Backed Gull	Not numerous but nest widely on Rocher Percé and the island. Seen from cruises.	April to October	Certain
Harlequin Duck	Seasonal in Baie de Percé and near the island.	Spring and autumn	Occasional
Double-Crested Cormorant	A few on the island, but many more and easier to spot at Rocher Percé.	April to October	Certain

Great Cormorant	Less abundant than Double-Crested Cormorants; can be seen on the island near Chemin du Roy.	April to October	Uncertain
Northern Harrier	This bird of prey is a regular visitor to the island. Can be seen near Chemin du Roy.	August	Occasional
Bald Eagle	This large bird of prey frequents the Les Colonies area and Chemin du Roy.	Spring	Occasional

Note: Île Bonaventure is accessible only by boat, from the opening of the park (late May) to mid-October.

Razorbill

These birds, which resemble a penguin, dive from the surface; they usually only go a few metres down but can reach 120m. They can hold an astonishing nine little fish in their beaks at once.

Razorbills were extirpated from Iceland in 1844 by excessive unregulated hunting. In the park, by contrast, the population is rising and is estimated at 1,300 pairs on Île Bonaventure and more than 100 couples on Rocher Percé.

Atlantic Puffin

The puffin's large, colourful triangular beak, sharply contrasting with its black back and white belly, earns it the nickname of "sea parrot." Even though it is much more strongly associated with the Mingan Archipelago National Park Reserve of Canada in the Côte-Nord, it can occasionally be seen on the rocky coast of Île Bonaventure. Despite its scarcity, it becomes easier to see in mid-August after the murres and razorbills have left.

Much more adapted to underwater swimming, its short wings make for laborious takeoffs and landings. It must maintain a very fast rate of 300 to 400 wingbeats per minute to maintain flight. It dives as far as 60m deep to feed on capelin, sand lances, or crustaceans such as shrimp.

Black-Legged Kittiwake

Though its white belly, grey wings, and yellow beak resemble those of its cousin and predator the Gull, the Black-Legged Kittiwake is more agile and much smaller. It teems over the small ledges of the cliffs, with a count finding more than 23,000 pairs on Île Bonaventure and 1,400 pairs on Rocher Percé.

This seabird feeds on little fish and plankton from the surface of the sea. Groups follow fishing boats to feed on fish waste.

Gulls

Most people are familiar with the big white gulls that abound on the seashore, opportunistically scavenging or feeding on eggs and chicks. As they float too well to swim underwater, they feed at low tide.

At Percé, gull populations have sharply declined since the closure of various fisheries. They are still less numerous on Île Bonaventure.

Two main species are seen. The solitary Great Black-Backed Gull is distinguished by its black wings and back. The Herring Gull, nesting in small colonies, has black-tipped grey wings instead.

Cormorants

Cormorants are easy to recognize as small groups of long-necked black birds. They can be seen at the summit of Rocher Percé and on the cliffs along the banks.

These coastal birds dive under the surface to feed on fish and invertebrates. Most are Double-Crested Cormorants, alongside a few Great Cormorants, which are larger.

Harlequin Duck

This sea duck is named for its resemblance to a clown in the *commedia dell'arte*, who wears a colourful, white-striped costume and face paint. The Harlequin Duck can be immediately recognized by the white ovals on its cheeks. It frequents rocky coasts, feeding on insects and marine invertebrates.

Threatened with extirpation in the 1990s, the Harlequin Duck is still considered vulnerable. A rehabilitation plan has helped, but the Atlantic population is still less than 1,000 individuals.

Overview of Activities

There are so many things to do in the national park that you could stay here for days without ever running out. The season runs from the third week of May to mid-October. However, as several activities are only offered for a shorter period, check before you set out.

Attractions

■ Percé

La Neigère

The Charles Robin Company used this building to store herring and mackerel on blocks of ice covered in sawdust, as bait for angling for cod.

Today, La Neigère houses the park's Information Kiosk and Boutique Nature store, an essential stop before you

The Witch of Percé Rock

Once, a Mi'kmaq orphan lived in a cave in the Escuménac cliffs. When she prepared fish, she gave the scraps to her friends the birds, and so was known as Shenandaha, the bird girl.

Enchanted with her beauty and kindness, a young man named Pentagoët fell in love with her and gave her a coat of caribou hide and an embroidered bracelet of porcupine hair. After some hesitation, Shenandaha accepted the gifts as engagement presents, and promised to give her answer at the next full moon.

Unfortunately, Gouhou-Gouhou, the witch of the great rock, had overheard their conversation. In love with Pentagoët herself and determined to stop the marriage, she managed to capture Shenandaha by luring her with an injured bird, then imprisoned her in a dark hole dug right into the great rock.

The full moon came, and Pentagoët could not find his beloved anywhere. He was distraught.

While he brooded, Gadalou, a good witch who had always loved him like a son, came to him. Divining that his beloved was imprisoned in the rock, Gadalou told the boy to set out as soon as possible, giving him magic shells to protect him.

As Pentagoët walked onto the great rock, a trap opened under his feet and he fell into a hole, finding himself imprisoned with his beloved.

He threw one of the magic shells against the wall, and a huge explosion blew the walls off the trap. Pentagoët and Shenandaha saw the sea on either side. An arch had been formed, piercing the rock through and through, and so it has been from that day to this.

head to Rocher Percé or Île Bonaventure. By asking questions and chatting with the park wardens, you will get a good overview of the attractions.

Le Chafaud

Built on scaffoldings (*échafaudages*), Le Chafaud was used for processing dried salt cod. The production line, which also extracted cod livers, occupied the ground floor, while the upper floor was used to store fish and merchandise.

The building is now a Discovery Centre, explaining the processing of cod as well as the history of the cod fishery and the Channel Islands companies that ran it. Exploring the park begins with the exhibition here (photos, illustrations, videos, and commentaries). It also describes how the Gaspé Peninsula and Rocher Percé were formed.

The 30-minute film on seabirds is also a good introduction to your visit to Île Bonaventure. A self-guided visit also gives a good overview of the island's flora and the local sea mammals.

La Saline

La Saline was once a warehouse for salt from the salt marshes of Cadiz in Spain, used to salt the cod at Le Chafaud.

In the high season, talks are presented here every evening, on whales, seals, seabirds, and the history of the region.

La Cantine

La Cantine was once a 300-man dormitory for the employees of the Charles Robin Company, fishers and cod processing workers. Employees were recruited as far away as Bas-Saint-Laurent to work in the fishery. Today, the building houses the park's administration office.

■ Rocher Percé

At low tide, you can walk from the mainland to Rocher Percé, looking at cast-up shells and even the occasional crab scuttling under a rock. However, it is forbidden to venture too close to the rock itself, as eroded chunks of rock can fall off.

In high season, don't miss the "Petit Peuple de la Mer" activity on the beach around the rock at low tide, visitors watch as a park warden handles local marine organisms kept in aquariums. You will learn how these ocean dwellers adapt to the tides.

Warning: Rocher Percé sheds 300 tonnes of rock per year. It is dangerous to walk near it. Access to the rock is prohibited to self-guided visitors, but is allowed with a guide during the high season. There is no access in the low season.

■ Île Bonaventure

Maison Le Boutillier

A visit to this now-restored house is a trip back in time. It once belonged to the manager of a fishing station run by Le Boutillier Brothers, a Channel Islands cod company that set up shop on the island in the 19th century.

Painted white and red to imitate the whitewash and bull's blood once used instead, this plush residence was ideal for receiving (and impressing) important visitors. The manager lived here alone, without his family.

Four other fishing company buildings stand around the residence. An old warehouse with a bull's-eye window was used to store dried salt cod, to be taken by schooner to the distribution centre at Paspébiac.

Paspébiac was also the source of the pre-cut, ready-to-assemble lumber used to build the warehouse. The numbers are still visible on the beams and planks! The warehouse now hosts Resto des Margaux.

An old cantina that served as a dormitory for company workers is now an information kiosk. Finally, the two other Le Boutillier Brothers buildings were milk houses, used for warehousing milk and other perishable products.

Nearby stand four more recent houses, which once belonged to island residents. The Mauger house (1940) now hosts a Boutique Nature store.

Activities

■ Cruises

Offered by park concessionaires, cruises commented by park wardens always delight passengers. The boat ranges along the foot of the cliffs, where tens of thousands of seabirds wheel and flock, and seals show off. Other cruises offer whale-watching.

A 2h lobster discovery cruise is available from July to mid-August. Leaving from Quai de Percé, the boat brings visitors off L'Anse-à-Beaufils, where a real lobster fisherman pulls up his pots while providing a colourful commentary.

■ Hiking

Although the national park is not very large, there are still 15km of trails on Île Bonaventure. Some follow the trails used by the first inhabitants, while others have been set up to take advantage of prime viewpoints and various natural settings.

From the service area, the trails converge on the ultimate attraction, the gannet colony. Some 120,000 birds nest at your feet, without even taking fright or flying off.

Master Fox

You may see one or two foxes as you walk the trails. They are used to visitors and are not fierce. However, you should not approach or feed them.

There are only a few on the island, which though small is enough to support them. When they aren't lucky enough to catch an abandoned chick, they feed on hares and small rodents.

Les Mousses

Length: 3.5km
Time: 1h15
Level: easy

The Mousses trail, leading past some rocky outcroppings, is a quiet path through a regenerating boreal forest.

To the east, on the coast, two lookouts provide a view of the bay of Saint-Georges-de-Malbaie and the points of the Gaspé coast.

Les Colonies

Length: 2.8km
Time: 45min
Level: easy

This is the busiest trail, leading to the gannet colonies. As the trail rises 130m, benches are offered to allow visitors to rest awhile and admire the view.

The trail passes through grassland, a regeneration area, and boreal forest. The .exuberant variety of wildflowers and other plants creates a vast palette of lovely colours and scents.

Park wardens are on site at the gannet colony to offer information on the birds' behaviour and life cycle.

Chemin du Roy

Length: 4.9km
Time: 1h30
Level: easy

This trail is named for the road that links the islanders' former houses, the remnants of a tiny community of fishers and farmers from the last century.

Leaving from the Les Colonies area, the route offers superb viewpoints over the sea. Keep your eyes open—you might spot a whale offshore.

Black-legged kittiwakes, razorbills, and black guillemots nest on the cliffs, especially around Baie des Marigots. It's worthwhile to stop on the beach to admire the landscape.

Past Baie des Marigots, the trail leads out of the forest onto the grassland, once farmland and pasture where the 19th-century fishers built their houses and buildings.

The trail runs past a few ruined houses that once belonged to colonists with evocative names such as Duval, Wall, or Maloney—names that can now be seen in the modest cemetery.

With time, nature has gradually erased the traces of the past, but not so much as to obliterate it entirely. In a regenerating area, native plants flourish in the sunlight and colonize the old farmlands. Field birds occasionally brighten the walk.

Paget

Length: 3.7km
Time: 60min
Level: easy

The Paget trail crosses a spruce forest before ending at the Visitors Centre. Unlike the other trails, there are no blackflies or mosquitoes to annoy you, as the local rock (conglomerate) prevents water from accumulating. Many of the rocks are red, tinted by iron oxide.

Tip

The best route is out by the Les Mousses trail and back by Chemin du Roy. If you still feel like walking, go ahead and walk one of the other paths.

Practical Information

Lodging

Percé

From a luxury hotel to the plainest motel and camp-grounds, Percé offers every level of accomodations, with views of the sea and Rocher Percé. Why not stay here for a few days or even for your entire trip? You're in no danger of being bored.

Dining

Île Bonaventure

In the service zone, Resto des Margaux offers salads, sandwiches, and its famous *"soupe du pêcheur."* Snacks can be prepared to go upon request. A Boutique Nature store sells useful items. While waiting for the boat back, shop for a souvenir from the Parcs Québec collection.

La Colonie

If you didn't bring anything to eat or drink while watching the gannets, there is a service centre to help you out.

Percé

In Percé, the buildings of the Charles Robin Company recall the turbulent period of the cod fishery. The old general store, red and white as usual, retains its period look, but now houses a food market. Also in the usual colours, the company barn, once used to supply employees' needs, now houses two restaurants.

The fishery manager's house is now an inn. Next to it is a restaurant in a huge building that housed employees during the fishing season. Percé offers both fine cuisine and more affordable family dining.

Equipment Rental

Percé

La Neigère houses both the Visitors Centre and a Boutique Nature store offering quality clothing and equipment from the Parcs Québec line.

In Percé, divers can find all the services they need to practise their sport. Guided sea kayak excursions visit Barachois (birds), the marine park area around Île Bonaventure (birds and seals), and around Rocher Percé.

Nearby

Percé

Beyond the national park, there are other grand open spaces to explore nearby. A network of 13km of foot trails crosses Mont Sainte-Anne and Mont Blanc. Levels: easy to intermediate. Guided tours in all-terrain vehicles are available in the Percé mountains with stops at Mont Sainte-Anne, the cave, or Pic de l'Aurore.

Shopping

A stroll through Percé can turn up any number of interesting finds, from sandstone gannets at a craft store to an exhibit on ornamental gardens and water gardens in a former agricultural school run by the Clerics of Saint Viateur.

Outings

From a glass of wine on a terrace to an evening at a show, there's plenty to do at night. A visit to an authentic general store is a chance to travel back in time to the beginning of the last century in the midst of the cod fishery.

Association touristique de la Gaspésie
☎ 1-800-463-0323
www.tourisme-gaspesie.com/en

PARC NATIONAL DE MIGUASHA

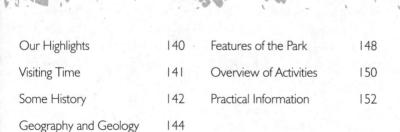

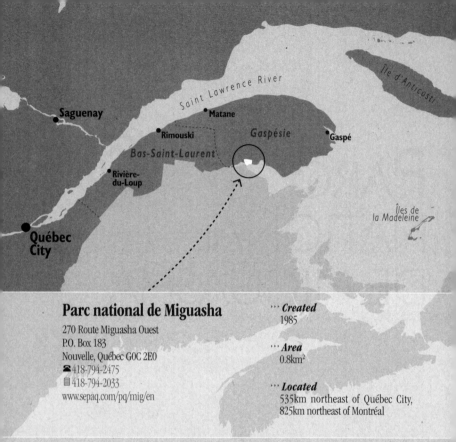

Parc national de Miguasha

270 Route Miguasha Ouest
P.O. Box 183
Nouvelle, Québec G0C 2E0
☎ 418-794-2475
📠 418-794-2033
www.sepaq.com/pq/mig/en

··· *Created*
1985

··· *Area*
0.8km²

··· *Located*
535km northeast of Québec City,
825km northeast of Montréal

Our Highlights

The unquestionable highlight of Parc national de Miguasha is the guided tour of the exhibition *From Water to Land* at the Natural History Museum, featuring dozens of fossil fish, invertebrates, and plants dug out of the park's cliff. This tour introduces visitors to the world of fossils, a journey 380 million years through time, before even the dinosaurs appeared, when the fish were still the only vertebrates on Earth, but some were getting ready to take their first steps on dry land...

Visiting Time

··· *One hour*

Use your time to follow the path along the cliff and admire the splendid view of the estuary of Rivière Ristigouche and the surrounding mountains. A 220-step staircase allows you to continue along the beach, where you can admire the cliff that holds the fossils of extinct fish.

You can also use the time to visit the permanent exhibit and discover what the Miguasha landscape looked like 380 million years ago. Take a few minutes to admire the fish fossils, which are among the finest in the world.

··· *A half-day*

A half-day is a better length of time in which to really soak up the magic of Parc national de Miguasha. You'll have the time to visit the exhibit and the beach to discover the fascinating world of paleontology, the study of fossils. Travelling exhibits on other interesting subjects are also presented. In the summer, talks are offered about the evolution of life on Earth and the history of the cliff and the fossil digs. The wardens' passion for their subject is unforgettable.

Have a snack at the park's Le Dévonien restaurant and check out the little treasures at the museum's L'Échoppe boutique before getting back on the road.

··· *A day or more*

Relax and take the time to do all the activities described below at your own pace. The museum's terrace offers an impressive view of the countryside, with dining tables and seats to lounge in while reading or enjoying the view. Two fully equipped guest houses can be rented for one night or longer. The sunsets are marvellous, and the environment is calm and peaceful, allowing you to enjoy the region's other sights while staying in an enchanting setting.

The smallest of Québec's national parks, Parc national de Miguasha distinguishes itself from all the rest of the Sépaq network by its chief attraction—the priceless fossils in its cliff. The site is a unique opportunity to discover the fascinating world of palaeontology, admiring and learning from 380-million-year-old fossils, so well preserved and lifelike that they amaze scientists and visitors alike. A guided tour of the park's Natural History Museum brings the fossils to life. It's all part of an enchanting natural setting, Pointe de Miguasha, whose wooded valleys and cliff overlook the estuary of Rivière Ristigouche.

Some History

The First Explorers

The Mi'kmaq Nation originally inhabited the region, with the first European settlers arriving in the 17th century. However, the history of the park doesn't really start until the first scientific visit.

The fossil treasures of Miguasha were discovered in 1842. Dr. Abraham Gesner, the Provincial Geologist of New Brunswick, was assigned by the colonial government to search for coal. He crossed from Dalhousie, New Brunswick, to Québec, hoping to make useful discoveries on this side of the Rivière Ristigouche estuary. Instead of coal, he discovered fossils—plants, fish, and the remains of what he thought was a turtle, but was in fact a species of fish very common in the cliff, *Bothriolepis canadensis*. He mentioned his discoveries in his 1843 report, but they were quickly forgotten.

In 1879, a team from the Geological Survey of Canada rediscovered the fossils of Miguasha while mapping the west of the Chaleur Bay region. Following the rediscovery, a series of expeditions were organized in 1880 and 1881; they collected numerous plant and fish fossils. These led to a spate of scientific publications on the fossils of Miguasha between 1880 and 1882.

Following these publications, foreign scientists, Americans and Europeans alike flocked to the area to collect fossils. Thousands of specimens were taken. In 1922, Erik Stensio, a renowned Swedish palaeontologist, collected as many as 1,200 specimens in nearly 30 tonnes of rock! Many foreign researchers relied on the help of local families, notably the Plourdes and the Landrys, for help on their digs.

Québec Discovers Its Own Riches

Québec scientists, however, did not begin to study Miguasha until 1937, when Brother Léo-G. Morin from University of Montréal and Father J.W. Laverdière from Laval University, visited the region and saw a roadside sign marked *Fossils for sale*. This sign led them to the Plourde family, who told them that foreign researchers were coming in droves to collect fossils from the cliff. Québec provincial authorities were quickly alerted. René Bureau of the Ministère des Mines was mandated to assemble a first Québec collection of Miguasha fossils and immediately took steps to protect the site. His efforts did not bear fruit right away, since the fossils were forgotten in the heat of the Second World War. However, it was thanks to Monsieur Bureau's efforts that the site was protected and the later history of Miguasha was made possible. In 2007, 70 years after René Bureau first visited, the fossil-bearing cliff was named Falaise René-Bureau.

Things started to come together in 1970, when the Quebec government purchased part of the cliff. The first museum was opened in 1978, and the conservation park was created in 1985. The hard work of a passionate team was richly rewarded in 1999 when the park received the status of a UNESCO World Heritage Site. Since then, the park has not stopped developing and growing in prominence. Researchers from around the world continue to flock to the site to study the fossils of Miguasha. A research chair in lower vertebrate palaeontology at Université du Québec à Rimouski has been under development since 2004 to facilitate research for local and foreign palaeontologists and spread information about the discoveries made from the fossils of Miguasha.

Geography and Geology

Geography

Parc national de Miguasha is located on the southern shore of the Gaspésie region, at the end of Chaleur Bay. Where the fresh water of Rivière Ristigouche meets the salt water of the bay, a headland advancing into the estuary forms Pointe de Miguasha. This peninsula, 25km west of Carleton-sur-Mer, is renowned throughout the region for the peaceful beauty of its landscapes. The park itself is located on the west side of the point, facing the magnificent Ristigouche estuary, and covers a thin strip along its famous fossil cliff.

Geological Time

The Earth is about 4.5 billion years old. By convention, geologists divide the history of the world into various periods. The longest of these is the Precambrian period, from the formation of the Earth to about 543 million years ago (MYA). The first life forms emerged during this period. The last 550 million years are divided into shorter geological periods during which life grew in diversity and complexity and spread throughout the world. The Devonian is the fifth geological period, running from about 417 to 354 MYA. For comparison, another, more famous geologic period, the Jurassic, occurred between 206 and 114 MYA.

Geology

The geological history of Pointe de Miguasha is intimately linked to that of the Appalachians. This mountain chain extends thousands of kilometres through eastern North America and forms the backbone of the Gaspé Peninsula. The Appalachians were formed in several stages extending over a very long period of time. The Gaspésie section of the mountain chain was formed between the Middle Ordovician and Middle Devonian periods, between 470 and 370 million years ago.

At the end of the Devonian period, the landscape of what would one day be Gaspésie was dominated by the young Appalachians. Today rounded and worn by weather (wind, rain) and glaciers, they were then quite a different sight. They probably resembled today's Rockies or Alps, with sharp peaks reaching several thousand metres in altitude. Their progressive erosion over hundreds of millions of years shaped them into their current forms. Material scoured from the Appalachians after the end of the Devonian was carried by rivers and streams to the lowlands. These sediments (pebbles, sand, and clay) were deposited on plains and in lakes around the mountains. As they accumulated, they became compacted and gradually formed sedimentary rocks.

The rocks within Parc national de Miguasha are of this type, formed by the erosion of the Appalachians. Originally

Parc national de Miguasha   -   Geography and Geology   -   Geology deposited in horizontal layers, the sedimentary strata have been somewhat crumpled by later tectonic deformations. Visitors looking at the cliffs are left speechless imagining the power of the geological forces capable of deforming rock strata tens of metres thick. Three geological formations are exposed on the cliff, dating from the Devonian and Carboniferous periods (354 to 290 million years ago), the first phases of the erosion of the Appalachians.

Fleurant Formation

At the base of the cliff is the oldest geological formation visible in the park, the Fleurant Formation. This formation probably dates from the Late or Upper Devonian period. It consists of conglomerate, a type of sedimentary rock made up of small stones and pebbles of various sizes suspended in a finer matrix such as sand. The same type of deposit can be found in certain present-day freshwater waterways, such as fast-flowing rivers: a stiff current is needed to move such stones. The Fleurant Formation is therefore thought to be the result of a sedimentary deposit left by a fast river flowing down from the young Appalachians.

Escuminac Formation

Just on top of the Fleurant Formation, and therefore slightly younger than it, is the Escuminac Formation. With a total thickness of 117m, this formation makes up most of the cliff. Its strata are not perfectly horizontal, but slightly slanted, like a deck of cards slid out on a table, and are spread out over the cliff up to 30m high. These deposits of clay, silt, and sandstone have yielded the fossils that have won this site its world renown and led to the creation of the park. At around 380 million years old, this formation is a window on the past, a unique chance to study life at a crucial stage of its evolution frozen in rocks that have survived nearly 400 million years of geological history.

Fossilization

A fossil is the remains or traces of a past organism. It can be part of an organism itself, such as a shell, bones, or hair, or evidence of its activities, such as a burrow or footprint. For a living thing to be preserved as a fossil, certain conditions must be met. The organism must be quickly buried to preserve it from scavengers and the elements. It may be buried under sediments, mud, and sand at the bottom of a body of water. Next, the organism must be preserved from bacterial decomposition; this is reduced or halted in the absence of oxygen, which many bacteria need to decompose an organism. The floor of the Devonian Miguasha estuary is thought to have been oxygen-poor, at least occasionally, explaining the exceptional state of some of the fossils.

Over time, the progressive accumulation of new sedimentary layers compacts the old ones and forces water out. Eventually, chemical reactions bind sedimentary particles together to make up rock. Mineral structures in organisms, such as teeth, shells, bones, and scales, are usually the best preserved. If fossil-bearing rocks are spared by erosion, they may be found by chance during digs.

Scientists believe that 380 million years ago, Miguasha was a transition environment between a vast river rising in the Appalachians and a salt-water sea. Québec was then a few degrees south of the Equator, and Miguasha had a hot, humid equatorial or tropical climate. The brackish waters of the estuary teemed with a rich fauna of strange fish and invertebrates such as worms, tiny crustaceans, and eurypterids, aquatic scorpions up to a metre long! The shores of the estuary hosted other invertebrates such as millipedes and smaller, but still frighteningly large, scorpions. These land organisms lived in undergrowth made up of small swamp plants and trees up to 10m high, with foliage like that of ferns. These trees, thought to be transitional forms between true ferns and seed-bearing plants like conifers and flowering plants, were the first forests the world ever knew.

A true tropical ecosystem flourished then in Miguasha on the edge of a vast estuary whose only traces

Parc national de Miguasha - Geography and Geology - Escuminac Formation

today are the accumulated sediments and the organisms who died there. From time to time, an organism's body would become trapped in the sediments that accumulated in the estuary, whether as steady, regular deposits or sudden, massive underwater landslides.

Bonaventure Formation

Finally, at the top of the cliff and forming the surface of Pointe de Miguasha, is the Bonaventure Formation. Lying on top of the other two formations, it provides a distinctive red colour contrasting with the rest of the cliff's grey tones. Dating from the Early Carboniferous period, it consists of alternating conglomerates, sandstone, and clay. The Bonaventure Formation is much larger than the other two, ranging over nearly the whole south coast of Gaspésie from Percé to Miguasha. This large sedimentary expanse was created by sedimentation in the criss-crossed waterways of a huge alluvial plain at the foot of the aging Appalachians. The reddish tint is due to oxidized iron ore, revealing that the sediment was in sporadic contact with air. This particularity of the Bonaventure Formation is the origin of the area's name "Miguasha" comes from a Mi'kmaq word meaning "red earth."

Features of the Park

Parc national de Miguasha's size is the only small thing about it. It distinguishes itself by its exceptional fossil heritage, which it showcases with a range of activities.

Fossils

The Escuminac Formation is teeming with fossil specimens of terrestrial and aquatic invertebrates, fish, and plants. More than 18,000 fossils have been recovered since the first digs in 1897, of which more than half are in the national collection of the park's Natural History Museum. The rest are held by numerous prestigious museums, including New York's American Museum of Natural History and the Muséum national d'Histoire naturelle in Paris, as well as various universities such as McGill, Laval, and Harvard. The Miguasha fossils have been used in many international research projects, but the cliff is far from finished revealing all of its secrets. Some 500 new specimens per year are discovered by the digging teams.

Each new find opens up new research possibilities, especially given the exceptional state of conservation that many are found in. While many fossil sites offer only disjointed fragments, the exceptional quality of Escuminac Formation fossils allows research that is otherwise impossible. Whole specimens, sometimes even conserved in 3D, are at the same time fonts of information for palaeontologists and natural works of art that amaze visitors.

International Recognition

The specimens yielded by the site allow the reconstruction of a turning point in the history of life on Earth, the Devonian Period or "Age of Fishes." The origin of the first forests, the diversification of land arthropods such as scorpions, spiders, and millipedes, the appearance and disappearance of numerous groups of fish, and the evolution of fish into the first groups of four-footed vertebrates, the tetrapods, are all crucial steps clearly represented in the Miguasha fossil record. As the world's best representative of this geological period, Parc national de Miguasha received the prestigious title of UNESCO World

Heritage Site in 1999, one of 14 in Canada and the second in Québec.

A National Research Centre

Such a significant fossil heritage naturally attracts the international palaeontological community. Each year, numerous scientists visit the park to do research. They are given access to the national collection of fossils from the cliff, a preparation laboratory, and a research facility with cutting-edge scientific equipment. The discoveries made are then shared directly with visitors through a continually updated education program. This desire for scientific communication and popular education has resulted in the creation of Québec's only province-run natural history museum.

Overview of Activities

The park's Natural History Museum is open year-round, but it is at its liveliest and offers the most activities in the summer.

Discovery Activities

■ **Guided Tour of the Exhibit**
   From Water to Land

Education has always been a priority for Parc national de Miguasha since the first museum opened in 1978. People can visit the exhibit independently, using the detailed interpretive panels, but a guided tour is the best way to really understand and appreciate the history preserved by the fossil record. Lasting about 1h30, the visit is led by enthusiastic and knowledgeable wardens who guide visitors on a trip through time to the key moment when the first tetrapods, evolved from Devonian fish, were preparing to take their first tentative steps on land.

The guided tour begins with a description of what scientists believe the Miguasha ecosystem looked like 380 million years ago, aided by a huge, magnificent mural by local artist François Miville-Deschênes. The visit continues through sections dealing with the formation of fossils, the history of the site, and the palaeontological process. However, the heart of the visit comes later, when you meet the fish species, some very strange ones indeed, that inhabited the Miguasha estuary in the Devonian period. Each of these species has something to teach about the process of speciation, evolution, and extinction. In particular, you'll see *Eusthenopteron foordi*, nicknamed the Prince of Miguasha, and its cousin *Elpistostege watsoni*, which were among the transitional forms between fish and tetrapods.

The guided tour concludes outside, where you can walk down to the beach to admire the cliff, the last resting place of the fossilized animals in the exhibit. The warden will offer interesting information about the cliff's geology and the digs. Finally, you'll see the site of the systematic digs, affectionately called the "slave pit." You might have the chance to chat with the researchers working there, who are often eager to talk about their work and share their latest finds.

■ Summer Talks

During the summer, a series of talks reveals other fascinating subjects on the evolution of the Universe and life on Earth. Lasting about 1h each, they discuss such subjects as the big bang, the appearance of life, the reign of the dinosaurs, the evolution of mammals, the adventure of the human species, and the use of genetics in studying the origins of humans, all at a level that everyone can appreciate. All these subjects help to understand the place that the Miguasha fossils play in the grand history of the Universe and life on our planet.

■ Temporary Exhibits

Each year, travelling scientific exhibits are presented in the temporary exhibition room. By turns scientific and artistic, these exhibits allow visitors to deepen their knowledge of geology and palaeontology. The rest of the year, the room presents exhibits of visual arts.

■ L'Évolution de la Vie Trail

This 1.9km-long trail, suitable for inexperienced hikers, runs through the woods above the fossil cliff. Numerous lookouts offer a marvellous panoramic view of Rivière Ristigouche. Interpretive panels summarize the Earth's 4.6-billion-year history. At the far end, a staircase continues down to the beach to allow you to admire the fossil strata. Although tolerated, bathing is not recommended as there is no lifeguard on duty.

Practical Information

Lodging

The park owns two guest houses, fully equipped with dishes, bedding, etc., allowing you to enjoy the beauty of Miguasha and its region. Maison de l'Estuaire can house up to 10 people, while Maison Parent can sleep 6. You will also find campgrounds, bed and breakfasts, and an inn, all within 3km and 10km from the park.

Dining

In the park, Le Dévonien restaurant serves delicious meals, including a choice of excellent home-made breakfasts and lunches. A choice of fast food–type meals (fries, hot dogs, poutine) is also available, as well as Gaspésie's delicious local seafood sandwiches and salads. You can enjoy your meals in the dining room or the magnificent panoramic terrace. Picnic tables are scattered around the site if you prefer to eat al fresco.

Near the park, a few home-style restaurants and snack bars welcome you too. In Carleton-sur-Mer, 25km from the park, you can enjoy more refined dining that showcases local products.

Shopping

In the park's museum, the L'Échoppe boutique offers a selection of the park's brand products, such as clothing and hats. However, the vast collection of fossils, minerals, and rocks are the real attraction. Jewellery made from a very rare gemstone, ammolite, is sold. Ammolite is the fossilized remains of the shells of ammonites, invertebrates extinct for 65 million years. The boutique also offers numerous unique works by local craftspeople, as well as casts of some of the most celebrated fish fossils of Miguasha, made on site and available nowhere else.

Nearby

Fans of the great outdoors can enjoy numerous nearby pedestrian trails and cycling paths, part of the Québec-wide Route Verte. From Parc national de Miguasha, the Shoolbred trails are available for hikers and cyclists, while the Carleton-Maria trails offer a wide variety of routes from beginner to expert levels in a large 30km network. Breathtaking views of the mountains and sky await hikers.

For history buffs, the Battle of the Ristigouche National Historic Site of Canada at Pointe-à-la-Croix presents the archaeological explorations of the wreck of a French frigate, *Le Machault*, in Rivière Ristigouche. This was the site of the last major battle of New France, in 1760.

Those who enjoy exceptional views shouldn't miss Mont Saint-Joseph and Oratoire Notre-Dame-du-Mont-Saint-Joseph in Carleton-sur-Mer. Guided tours of the oratory are offered, and you can admire the beauty of the landscape from the top of a 555-m-high mountain! You can reach the summit on foot or by car.

Those visiting in the month of May can enjoy activities organized by the town of Nouvelle as part of the Festival de la famille. Anglers can also pit their wits against Rivière Nouvelle, which hosts weakfish and Atlantic salmon.

FORILLON NATIONAL PARK OF CANADA

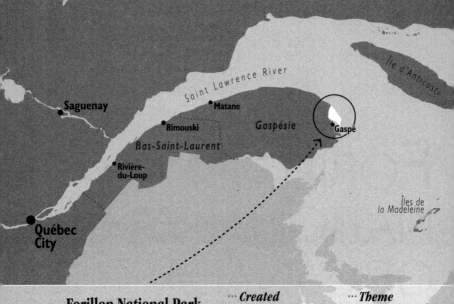

Forillon National Park of Canada
(see map p. 208)

122 Boulevard Gaspé
Gaspé, Québec G4X 1A9
☎ 418-368-5505 or 1-888-773-8888
🖶 418-368-6837
www.pc.gc.ca/forillon

⋯ *Created*

1970

⋯ *Area*

245km², coastline area 4.4km² from Cap des Rosiers (north) to Petit-Gaspé (south)

⋯ *Theme*

Harmony between man, land, and sea

⋯ *Located*

890km northeast of Montréal and 660km northeast of Québec City

Our Highlights

⋯ *The mountain*

The North Area of the park offers the most spectacular geological sights, with the sheer cliffs and long pebble beaches of Cap Bon Ami. The hiking trail to Mont Saint-Alban offers close-up views of the cliffs and an overview of Forillon's mountainous landscape.

The South Area gives visitors access to Cap Gaspé, the farthest tip of the Gaspé and Forillon peninsulas, located in a majestic natural setting. The lower south coast bears the marks of erosion and shows off the different layers of rock built up over the eons.

··· *The sea*

The gentler relief of the South Area provides several ways to get to Baie de Gaspé, an arm of the sea to which the whole region's history is intimately tied. This side is also the departure point for sea kayaking and sea mammal watching.

In the North Area, the endless Gulf of St. Lawrence, which is more than 100km wide at this point, contrasts strongly with the view of Baie de Gaspé to the south. This area is the departure point for an interpretive cruise.

Presqu'île de Penouille distinguishes itself with its long sandy beach, low relief and salt marsh.

··· *History*

The whole South Area of the park is profoundly marked by the history of the fishery, the key to survival for all those who lived on this forbidding coast from the 18th century on. In Grande-Grave, several historical buildings bear witness to this period, which only drew to a close at the end of the 1960s. A whole range of interpretive activities and presentations help visitors understand those bygone days.

Visiting Time

··· *One hour*

North Area

Visit the Interpretation Centre, stop at the Cap-Bon-Ami lookout, and have a stroll along the shore.

South Area

Visit Grande-Grave and L'Anse-Blanchette, location of the Hyman & Sons store and the Blanchette homestead. The short footpath between the two sites gives an overview of the coastal geology and the shingle beaches (*graves* in archaic French), as well as the opportunity to spot seabirds and shorebirds.

Penouille

Hike the Pointe de Penouille trail and its beach, admiring the wonderful flora, shells, and birds.

···*A half-day*

North Area

- Visit the Interpretation Centre
- Stop at the Cap-Bon-Ami lookout and beach
- Hike the Mont-Saint-Alban trail

South Area

- Visit Grande-Grave and L'Anse-Blanchette
- Visit L'Anse-aux-Amérindiens
- Hike or cycle to Cap-Gaspé
- Combine both areas
- Visit the Interpretation Centre or Cap-Bon-Ami lookout and beach
- Visit Grande-Grave and L'Anse-Blanchette

Penouille

Hike to Pointe de Penouille and enjoy the view, then swim and picnic on the beach at the end of the trail (2km).

···*A day or more*

North Area (day 1)

- Visit the Cap-des-Rosiers lighthouse
- Visit the Interpretation Centre
- Take an interpretive cruise
- Picnic at the Cap-Bon-Ami lookout and stroll along the beach
- Hike the Mont-Saint-Alban trail
- Camp in the North Area

South Area (day 2)

- Visit Grande-Grave and L'Anse-Blanchette
- Hike or cycle to Cap-Gaspé
- Have lunch at the recreation centre
- Choice of excursion: sea mammal watching or sea kayaking
- Camp in the South Area

Or a combination of the two half-day itineraries listed above.

Y ou start to smell the gentle tang of the salt air. The lapping of the sea barely drowns out the birdsong, and people's voices blend into a sweet melody. You find a tiny spot between the mountains and the sea… No mistake, you've arrived in Forillon.

Despite the great distances separating Gaspésie from Québec's population centres, the wide peninsula pointing into the Atlantic between the Gulf of St. Lawrence and Chaleur Bay has captivated the imagination of wanderers since the age of discovery, and all the more so since the rise of tourism.

Created in 1970 as the first national park of Canada in Québec, Forillon's stunning landscape is the farthest reach of the Gaspé Peninsula into the sea. The park is home to hundreds of species of birds, a profusion of marine and land fauna, and amazing geological formations.

The park is divided into two areas, North and South, a few kilometres' drive apart; each has its own distinctive geography, history, and attractions. A third location, Pointe de Penouille in the centre of the park's southern coast, is a separate section all its own. The North Area faces the Gulf of St. Lawrence while the South Area faces Baie de Gaspé. Each of the two areas offers a campground and a Visitor Reception Centre, as well as different or complementary interpretation and outdoor activities. It would be difficult to see them both in a short period of time.

Forillon National Park of Canada

Some History

Human Habitation

■ Prehistory

Archaeological digs in Gaspésie and in the park itself suggest that humans have inhabited this area for thousands of years (9,000 years in Vallée de l'Anse-au-Griffon and 4,000 years at Penouille). As sites used by Aboriginal fishers and gatherers were only used seasonally, we have little information on the first inhabitants.

■ European Arrival

During the 15th century, when European cod-fishers and whalers were just starting to frequent the Gulf of St. Lawrence, Gaspésie was already inhabited by Aboriginal people of the Mi'kmaq nation, known as "Souriquois." Two other nations of the Algonquian language group lived in southwestern Gaspésie, the Maliseet and Etchemins.

The first "vacationers" to visit Gaspésie regularly were the Iroquois of the future Québec City region, who came to fish along the north coast of the peninsula. They were the nation that Jacques Cartier encountered in 1534 and met again at the future site of Québec City the following year.

The region of *Gachepay*, as Samuel de Champlain wrote it in 1603, was first visited and then occupied by fishers during the first few centuries of colonization; it also constituted an important stopping point for transatlantic navigation. (See the information box on Gaspé for more information on the early history of permanent settlement.)

Fishery

In the Forillon area, like elsewhere in Gaspésie, the cod fishery was dominated by companies from the Channel Islands, who held a pitiless oligopoly. The strategy all the large companies used was to set up a credit system that rendered workers completely economically dependent. Companies became both the sole employer and the exclusive supplier of essential goods. They determined resource prices and profited from the credit accumulated from the dried and salt cod the fishers sold them, resulting in total control.

Starting in 1777, a number of Channel Islands companies set up shop and prospered in Grande-Grave thanks to the exceptional quality of the fishery and the work of dozens of "engaged" men. The merchant William Hyman, whose memory is preserved at Grande-Grave in the park, arrived on Presqu'île de Forillon around 1845 and stayed more than 60 years. His business, Hyman & Sons, continued the traditional fishery until it went bankrupt in 1967.

The people of Forillon stayed trapped in this system and a conservative society they were unable to escape.

Creation of the Park

In 1970, the people of Forillon were thrust into the modern world, a shock cushioned by new government social programs. It was at this point that a federal-provincial agreement paved the way for Forillon National Park. Its creation required some 200 homes to be expropriated; most of the families moved in with family in nearby villages. This uprooting had different effects for different people, with some having their lives completely disrupted and others seeing it as an opportunity to leave behind a life of misery. The expropriation, still a delicate subject, has been the subject of numerous debates and ample media coverage.

Today, several families with roots in Forillon live near their ancestral homes. Far from burying their family history, Parks Canada preserves it by conserving natural diversity while commemorating the difficult life of those who had the strength, courage, and determination to live here.

Geography and Geology

Witness to the Evolution of the Earth

The landscapes of Forillon bear witness to the grandest ballet of all time, the impossibly slow and gradual evolution of the Earth itself. The movements of the Earth's crust, sliding, rippling, and upthrusting, have left their marks here, and one need not be a specialist to read their story in the rocks. The passage of time has carved out its signature in wind and rain, while the sea has added its part, sculpting the coastline into fantastic forms—ledges, grottoes, and dizzying cliffs.

Humans, too, have made their mark, building their nests as hundreds of thousands of birds have every year since time immemorial. Ploughing up the soil, drawing precious resources from the sea, and spreading cod over the beaches to dry in the sun, humankind marked the earth and changed its destiny, before finally protecting this incomparable land.

Geography

Forillon National Park of Canada occupies a mountainous peninsula, 36 km in length, extending like a finger into the Gulf of St. Lawrence. Similar in surroundings and shape to Cap Corse in Corsica, Pointe de Forillon is the far eastern mainland end of the great Appalachian mountain chain, which extends from Alabama to Newfoundland. With singular accuracy, Mi'kmaq called this region *Gespeg*, "land's end." Seen from the Gulf of St. Lawrence, the peninsula's relief is tilted southward, towards Baie de Gaspé, while the rock faces along its north shore can reach 200m in height. The peninsula narrows between Cap Bon Ami and Grande-Grave, forming a slender spit of land leading to the farthest point.

Created in 1970, this 22nd of Canada's national parks covers 244.8km², including a 4.4km² fringe of sea. It represents the natural region of the Notre Dame and Megantic Mountains as well as part of the Gulf of St. Lawrence marine region. The splendour of its contorted landscapes may not suggest bucolic harmony, but a deeper understanding of the land and its history reveals how humans, land, and sea have existed in a vital symbiosis. A profusion of flora and fauna defy the rigours of the land, giving it a unique identity that comes through in all of the park's numerous points of interest.

Geology

■ Reading the Landscape

Forillon National Park of Canada is an exceptional site for observing rock formations, a sort of calendar of geological time. Its exposed cliffs reveal an unusual phenomenon. Some ten distinct rock formations are sandwiched together in a series of parallel bands. This landscape was built up over two main periods, the Ordovician (460 million years ago) and Silurian-Devonian (395 to 420 million years ago) periods, during which successive layers of marine sediment piled up. Accordingly, the rock formations in the park reveal a long geological history, eloquently retelling the movements of the Earth's crust that created the Appalachian chain. The fossils found in the limestone strata, in addition to illustrating continental drift, also reveal the relative age of the rocks they are found in, the history of evolution, and the climatic conditions over the eons.

The impressive diversity and easy accessibility of Forillon's rock formations result in a landscape of exceptional geographical interest, protected by the park's mission of protecting, conserving, and enhancing the landscape.

■ Sharp Relief

The park occupies an area of steep coastal cliffs characteristic of this part of Gaspésie, so the rugged relief and exposed rock formations of the interior should not come as a surprise. The park's topography was sculpted by rocky strata tilted by tectonic activity to an angle of 20 to 30 degrees, creating a system of mountain ridges with southern faces sloping gently towards the sea and northern faces dropping off in the centre of the park with rock walls aligned parallel to the coast. The northern half of the park is more rolling and largely under 300m in altitude, divided by numerous narrow valleys, all oriented toward the Gulf of St. Lawrence.

Climate

The Presqu'île de Forillon enjoys a milder climate than one might expect so far north, largely because the sea cools the summers and moderates the severity of the winters. In Forillon, average July and January temperatures are 17°C and –10°C respectively, compared to 19°C and –10.6°C in

Gaspé

Forillon National Park of Canada is located within the municipality of Gaspé, the regional centre of Gaspésie. The town itself is located south of the park at the end of Baie de Gaspé, west of Presqu'île de Forillon.

■ History

The name "Gaspé" comes from the Mi'kmaq *Gespeg*, meaning "land's end." The history of New France began at Gaspé in 1534 with the first voyage of French explorer Jacques Cartier, considered the "discoverer" of Canada. Having sheltered in Baie de Gaspé, he planted a cross to take possession of the land in the name of the King of France, giving Gaspé the title of "cradle of Canada."

However, it was not until the 18th century that a permanent settlement was established on Baie de Gaspé. In 1765, following the British Conquest, retired English officers and soldiers were offered free land in Gaspé. They were later joined by 315 Loyalists in 1784. The arrival of these English-speaking colonists coincided with the creation of the commercial fishing empires. In 1833, John Le Boutillier entered the cod fishery, cod being abundant in Baie de Gaspé. In 1838, Le Boutillier Brothers (not to be confused with John Le Boutillier) joined the fish companies in the area, later becoming one of the two main dried cod exporting companies in Gaspésie, with Charles Robin and Co.

■ Transportation at the Heart of the Economy

The port of Gaspé became a free port between 1861 and 1866. Between 40 and 50 European ships stopped there annually, feeding the local economy. Remarkably, an Italian consulate was set up in Gaspé in 1862, quickly followed by American, Brazilian, Portuguese, and Norwegian ones. Gaspé was established as a municipality on December 9, 1873.

The railway reached the port in 1911. This would allow it, 50 years later, to become a shipping hub, benefiting from the key advantage of being able to stay open all year and shelter ships. It seemed possible that Gaspé would become a world-class port, but it was soon supplanted by Montréal and Halifax.

■ The Second World War

With the Second World War making the Gulf of St. Lawrence a strategic position, especially for the German navy whose submarines arrived in 1941, Gaspé became a key base for the Canadian military. A 3,000-man naval base was established at Sandy Beach to patrol the gulf, and strategic positions were established along the coast. Some traces of this period are still visible, such as the tunnels and coastal batteries of Fort-Péninsule at the southern entrance of the park, as well as the sites of Fort Prével and the Fort Ramsay naval base at Sandy Beach.

■ Today

In more recent memory, the government of Québec merged eleven municipalities into the city of Gaspé on December 24, 1970. It is now one of the largest municipalities in North America by area, at 1,440km², with 150km of coastline.

The creation of Forillon National Park of Canada, the first federal national park created in Québec, was one of the most significant events in the history of Gaspé. Recognizing the exceptional historical and ecological importance of Presqu'île de Forillon, the Parliament of Canada authorized numerous expropriations to protect the area. This wave of expropriations liberated 23,900ha of land, including 350 built properties and 1,690 wooded ones.

Today, Gaspé's industry centres on its excellent port, its rail and air transportation links, and its largely bilingual population.

Québec City and 21°C and –9.5°C in Montréal—a nearly negligible difference even though the cities are located far to the south and far inland. Annual average precipitation in Forillon is 100cm, compared to 92cm for southern Québec. The distance to the coast, the local topography, the altitude, and the prevailing winds greatly influence the climatic conditions within the park, often creating great variation from place to place.

Features of the Park

The infinite variety of the plant life in Forillon Park is distributed through a number of different biomes: forest, cliffs, alpine meadows, wild land, dunes, lakes, rivers, freshwater and salt marshes, and seashore.

One immediately notes that forest occupies the greatest share, covering 95% of the park's land area. The forest is representative of natural environments found throughout Québec—boreal coniferous forest and mixed forest. The Gaspesian climate favours fir forests with yellow birch, fir forests with white birch, and ferns.

Within these familiar environments, an even richer variety of plant life flourishes, encouraged by a host of factors such as superficial deposits, soil drainage, the numerous slopes, and exposure to sunlight and weather. No fewer than 63 forest communities and 696 plant species have been identified in Forillon Park. These include especially interesting plant communities such as the arctic alpine flora of the cliffs, the Penouille taiga, and the vegetation of the dunes and salt marshes.

Rare Plants

As the glaciers retreated, the sea cliffs of Gaspésie, especially in Forillon Park, were left with a population of plants usually found much further north. Some usually make their home in regions as far north as Baffin Island or the Yukon, or in the mountains of Alberta and Oregon. The alpine meadows of Cap Gaspé, like the talus and rock walls of the limestone cliffs exposed to the storms of the Gulf, are home to some 115 alpine or arctic plant species. Some 30 of these species, many of them rare, allow us to retrace events, such as the last ice age, which sculpted the landscape of Forillon and all of Québec. Some of these species only number a few dozen or a few hundred specimens in the park, making them highly vulnerable and subject to extreme precautions to keep visitors from treading on them or, worse still, picking them. Picking any plant is prohibited in all national parks.

Penouille

Pointe de Penouille is home to unique plant communities, set apart by the instability of the shifting dunes, the siliceous sand, and the thickness of the organic soil. Among these communities is a taiga of isolated black spruce on lichen-covered ground, whose origins are still a mystery. A number of plants that grow on the edge of the sea or forest live together here, such as sand ryegrass, fireweed, beach pea, glasswort, poverty grass, and dozens of others.

The salt march near Penouille is another special type of habitat, hosting plants that have adapted to the brackish water and the play of the tides.

Wildlife Watching

Knowing the surprising richness of the forest and flora of Forillon Park and the highly complex environment created by the interplay of numerous natural factors, it is not surprising that these many ecological niches also host a vast diversity of wildlife. Animal species range from humble marine invertebrates to ungulates, seabirds, and majestic sea mammals.

Land Mammals

Although the influence of the sea is omnipresent throughout the narrow peninsula, Forillon Park is host to a mammal population typical of the boreal forest. The moose, largest of the park's land animals, is right at home in the rugged resinous forests and the old farmlands where it feeds on brush. Black bears, generally smaller than others elsewhere in Québec, also live here, as do many smaller mammals that contribute to ecological stability. These include beaver, red fox, coyote, lynx, snowshoe hare, porcupines, groundhogs, mink, stoats, eastern chipmunks, and red squirrels.

■ Along the Roads

Attentive drivers regularly spot bears, moose, and even beaver dams along Route 132 towards Cap-des-Rosiers. Remember, these are not teddy bears—they're wild animals, and even small bears can injure or kill. They should therefore be observed from a distance, such as a car parked on the shoulder. For safety's sake, avoid getting out of your car, and remember that if you see bear cubs, the mother is never far away and you are definitely not welcome.

Heat and insects spur moose to leave the woods and wander along or even on the highway. It is essential to beware of moose on the road, especially in the evening or at night. A moose only needs a second to run from the ditch onto the road. Collisions with moose are usually deadly, as their bodies are at windshield height.

Campgrounds are often visited by hare, groundhogs, and fat little porcupines. When walking the trails, you can easily spot where porcupines have been, as they eat bark, which they strip in large quantities from tree trunks, killing the trees.

Birds

Forillon National Park is a paradise for birdwatchers. The endless waters of the Gulf of St. Lawrence, besides fascinating visitors, give the park its distinctive character. The graceful flight of seabirds above the horizon, the background music of their calls, and the privilege of watching them soar free contribute greatly to the charm and magic of Forillon.

■ Seabirds

Certain species of seabirds are abundant in Forillon. A count in 1989 found that six of them (Black-Legged Kittiwakes, Double-Crested Cormorants, Herring Gulls, Great Black-Backed Gulls, Black Guillemots, and Razorbills) had populations of more than 25,000 individuals nesting on the peninsula's cliffs. A seventh species, the Common Eider, nests on the beach at the foot of the rock walls.

Forillon is the only place on the north shore of Gaspésie that hosts large seabird colonies, as the innumerable ledges formed by the strata of the cliffs create a choice habitat for these birds. The north shore of the Gaspésie is mainly composed of brittle shale that crumbles relatively easily, producing few useful nesting sites. The Forillon cliffs, on the other hand, are made of limestone and therefore form numerous, highly durable ledges. Only Île Bonaventure, to the south and some distance offshore, has larger bird colonies than Forillon.

The Harlequin Duck, a magnificent little seabird, is one of the best-known and most remarkable visitors to Forillon Park. Listed as threatened at the beginning of the 1980s, this brilliantly coloured duck nests over wide arctic areas, and stops at Forillon Park during its migration. Fond of diving into the turbulent waters near rocky coasts, it is right at home on the north side of the Presqu'île de Forillon.

■ Migration

Forillon is a strategic point on one of the great migration corridors of North America, the Atlantic route. It serves as a major crossroads, acting as a stopover for thousands of birds migrating north-south. Some hundred land birds and seabirds stop here, greatly increasing the diversity of observable species.

Seabirds come and go with the seasons. Each year, the spring migrations bring Double-Crested Cormorants, Black Guillemots, Black-Legged Kittiwakes, Razorbills, and gulls, drawn by attractive nesting sites and the abundance of food in the Gulf of St. Lawrence and Baie de Gaspé. The cliffs of Cap Bon Ami host the largest flocks during the nesting period, including thousands of kittiwakes.

Seabirds begin to leave their nests in early August, while most forest birds do not leave until September or October.

In winter, with the sea around the park remaining relatively ice-free, thousands of birds come to winter near the coasts. Noisy flocks of up to 6,000 Long-Tailed Ducks can be seen, as well as three species of scoters, Iceland Gulls, and Glaucous Gulls, which nest in the Far North.

■ Land Birds

In contrast to the exuberant cries and displays of the seabirds, the land birds are relatively discreet, though very abundant—225 species can be found in the park, 124 of which nest here. A profusion of small birds inhabit the fields and forests, mainly buntings, warblers, jays, magpies, and thrashers. These grasslands and woods are also great places to observe the 26 species of birds of prey that frequent the park, the most common of which are the Rough-Legged Hawk (during the migration season only), the Northern Harrier, and the American Kestrel.

Among the park's shorebirds is the Great Blue Heron, a stoic wading bird, which feeds in the marsh at Penouille. Others include Common Terns, Ospreys, and various species of sandpipers. Several birds of prey put in a second appearance in autumn.

■ Birdwatching Sites

North Area

Étang du Cap des Rosiers

Thanks to its proximity to the north shore, this freshwater pond occasionally attracts exceptional sights such as Glossy Ibises, Greater White-Fronted Geese, Least Bitterns, Ruddy Ducks, American Coots, and Soras. Another twenty exceptional species have also been observed elsewhere in the park.

Route du Banc

The former agricultural area between the Cap-des-Rosiers lighthouse and the foot of the cliffs offers excellent chances to see diurnal birds of prey.

Anse du Cap des Rosiers is an excellent spot to watch the cliff-nesting seabirds feed. This is the place to see the daring high dives of Northern Gannets and other diving birds.

Forillon Cliffs

A cruise to the foot of the Forillon cliffs is the very best way to experience the sights and sounds of the seabird colonies on the cliffs. The sight of thousands of Black-Legged Kittiwakes wheeling in the sky is worth the trip in itself.

Near Cap Gaspé, a few Northern Gannets from Île Bonaventure can sometimes be seen escorting the Panorama-Découverte tour boat.

Cap-Bon-Ami Lookout

From the Cap-Bon-Ami lookout near the parking lot, visitors can observe the cliff-dwelling seabirds. A good pair of binoculars will pick out the clouds of kittiwakes to the southeast, while the Herring Gull's nesting sites can easily be seen from the parking lot. A public telescope is installed on site.

South Area

Very different from the escarpments to the north, the south side of the peninsula consists of points and bays lined with pebble beaches. Between Petit-Gaspé and Cap-Gaspé, abandoned farms intermingle with conifer stands, attracting birds of prey and other land birds.

The Cormorants' Pass

As the inhabitants of the peninsula once did to get from Cap-des-Rosiers to Grande-Grave, Double-Crested Cormorants and Herring Gulls now use the narrow pass between Grande-Grave and Cap-Bon-Ami to feed in Baie de Gaspé. The best viewpoint is on the main road through Grande-Grave harbour.

Les Graves Trail

This popular area offers many interesting bird-watching sites. The trail, which hugs the points and bays of the coastline, leads to Cap-Gaspé, where numerous species such as Great Black-Backed and Herring Gulls, Double-Crested Cormorants, Common Eiders, and Black Guillemots can be seen. Public telescopes are available at L'Anse-aux-Amérindiens.

Penouille Area

The Penouille area is a favourite of amateur ornithologists as its myriad natural habitats bring together a great diversity of bird species. Along the sandy point, taiga gives way to sand dunes and salt marshes. Several forest, field, and shore species frequent the area, including the Northern Flicker, the Common Ringed Plover, and the Savannah Sparrow. The salt marsh at the north end attracts dabbling ducks such as Mallards and Teals, and waders such as the Great Blue Heron. Birds of prey are frequently seen in the salt marshes.

Vallée de L'Anse-au-Griffon

Protected by mountains, Vallée de L'Anse-au-Griffon enjoys a warm microclimate that adds deciduous trees to the mixed forest. This environment welcomes a number of familiar species such as Siskins, Red-Winged Blackbirds, American Robins, and Song Sparrows. The open lowlands are often overflown by birds of prey. The valley can be reached on foot, by bicycle, or on horseback from the entrances to the north and south of the park.

Marine Life

The meeting of sea and land at Forillon creates an ideal habitat for marine life, bringing together the advantages, including food sources, of both domains.

The park's coasts host marine invertebrates such as mussels, urchins, crabs, and lobsters, which occupy rocky or sandy seafloors. Lobster fishers, launching from the park's docks, still operate every summer on both coasts of the peninsula. The Baie de Gaspé shore, with its tidal pools, is particularly rich. Harbour seals, which breed here, and grey seals regularly come to rest on the rocky coasts. They can be spotted on rocky outcroppings a short distance offshore.

■ Seals

At the exit of the Petit-Gaspé campground in the South Area or on the southern beaches, don't be surprised to see a seal comfortably sitting on a rock just a few metres offshore, paying no attention to curious onlookers. The lookout east of the Cap-des-Rosiers lighthouse and the secondary highway along the St. Lawrence between the lighthouse and the North Area Interpretation Centre (Route du Banc) are the two best places to spot them. A sea kayak excursion from Grande-Grave also offers an exciting chance to meet seals resting nearby on the coast. The seals here seem less aggressive than elsewhere.

■ Whales

Seven species of whales frequent the food-rich waters around the park. Both the world's largest and smallest cetaceans live together here: the blue whale, the largest animal ever to have existed on Earth, and the common porpoise, which rarely exceeds 2m in length.

Whale-Watching Cruises

A whale-watching cruise is always an unforgettable experience, especially in the ideal whale feeding grounds around Forillon. Those who have never whale-watched will learn the delicious excitement of anticipation and the fateful moment of sighting. Whale lovers will find that the environment around Forillon is radically different from that in the St. Lawrence estuary, and might be fortunate enough to see one or two rare species not usually seen further up the river, such as the long-finned pilot whale. Certain species that stop here in their migration can also be seen earlier in spring and later in autumn than in the estuary.

Baie de Gaspé Cruises

An excursion on *Narval III*, a large 48-passenger alum-
inium-hull inflatable boat, lasts about 2h30 and features
a bilingual guide to teach passengers all about the local
sea mammals. This fast, stable boat operated by Croisières
Baie de Gaspé, an official concessionaire of Forillon Park,
speeds to observation zones when whale blow is seen
(even far off), to give passengers the chance to meet the
largest animals in the world. When the motors are stopped,
the sound of whale blow echoes like an explosion, and
passengers thrill to the sight of the backs of blue, fin, and
minke whales, or the ultimate treat, the tail of a humpback
or better yet a blue whale. The cruise is also a great way
to view the spectacular landscape of Forillon and Cap
Gaspé from off shore.

Departure from Grande-Grave dock
1 to 4 departures per day.
Rain gear provided. Dress warmly.
Reservations and information: ☎ 418-892-5500 or 1-866-617-5500
www.baleines-forillon.com

Overview of Activities

Forillon National Park of Canada is a favourite with outdoor lovers,
with its network of hiking, horseback riding, and mountain biking
trails. Besides playing on its beaches, water sport lovers can go underwater diving, snorkelling, sea kayaking, and whale-watching.

Discovery Activities

Forillon National Park of Canada
offers an exceptional number of
interpretive activities. Whether
autonomously, using informa-
tional tools, or guided by spe-
cialists, visitors can explore in
depth the harmony that reigns

in the park between humans, land, and sea. Interpretation activities begin in June and run to mid-October.

■ Visitor Reception Centres

L'Anse-au-Griffon and Penouille

At the park entrances on Route 132, the L'Anse-au-Griffon and Penouille Visitor Reception Centres offer visitors all the information and documentation they need.

In Penouille, on the south side of the park, the Visitor Reception Centre displays several interpretive panels on the points of interest on the sandy point. The park staff can help plant lovers or birdwatchers identify what they see, and inform visitors about the park's services.

Cap-des-Rosiers

Interpretation Centre (North Area)

The North Area Interpretation Centre offers a brief but complete account of the park's special characteristics. The permanent exhibit in the main hall gives an overview of the park's natural and human history. Aquaria display numerous living specimens of the park's sea life. A film is presented about an outdoor subject upon request. Staff are available to give information on all aspects of the park and the services offered nearby.

Recreation Centre (South Area)

Located near the campsite, this service centre serves vacationers' every need. Among its services are a heated pool, a wading pool, tennis courts, and playgrounds. A snack bar, dairy bar, and patio serve meals and snacks, and a convenience store, Internet access, and a boxed lunch service for picnickers are also available. An automatic laundry and detergent vending machine are located nearby.

Grande-Grave Heritage Site

In Grande-Grave, the Hyman & Sons store symbolizes the yoke under which the cod fishers suffered during a dark period in the history of Gaspésie. The splendidly preserved building and its excellent interpretation fascinate visitors. A footpath hugs the flowered seashore. A visit to the Hyman & Sons general store and warehouse helps visitors grasp the crucial importance of the cod fishery for Gaspésie and its people.

The ties between merchants and fishers and the international scope of the fisheries in an age when Europe depended on the Grand Banks and St. Lawrence River for its cod are accurately depicted.

L'Anse-Blanchette

Close by, the Blanchette family house and outbuildings seem frozen in time. The period reconstruction is convincing even for people who lived it. Visitors need merely look up to lose themselves in the magnificent natural setting of sea and cliffs, with long fields of fireweed shaking in the wind. The life of the fishers and farmers and their families was often harsh, but they lived their scarce pleasures to the fullest and were deeply attached to their corner of the world. Guides in period costumes reenact the daily lives of the families who made their home at "land's end."

■ Cultural Interpretation

The many interpretive activities Forillon Park offers give visitors of all ages the chance to get to know the park's environment and history in a fun and accessible way. Theatre pieces portray real historical characters who played central roles in local life, while informal presentations let the whole family learn and have fun. Park staff cheerfully adapt each show to their audience, leaving behind the overly pedantic approach that used to prevail in national parks. The park's interpretive activities are free.

Human Habitation on Presqu'île de Forillon

Visitors to the Presqu'île de Forillon are overwhelmed by the majestic natural landscape. However, especially to the south, houses, cemeteries, roads, a church, and docks appear, making up what once

Grande-Grave

The word grave has been used since the 18th century to designate a pebble beach where fishers laid out their cod catch to dry in the sun. Later, grave became a place name indicating the whole area where cod was dried, including buildings. The name *Grande-Grave* commemorates the cod export industry that once went on here.

L'Ombre de l'épervier, a Novel and Television Series

The saga *L'Ombre de l'épervier*, by Gaspesian author Noël Audet (1938-2005), was adapted for television in 1998. This sweeping historical panorama, rich in emotions, was produced by Robert Favreau, who co-wrote the script with Guy Fournier. Thirteen episodes were produced, starring two of Québec's best actors, Luc Picard and Isabel Richer. The quality of the series and the strength of the actors earned numerous prizes. The novel itself, published by Éditions Québec Amérique, has sold more than 75,000 copies.

The extraordinary landscape of Forillon is the backdrop for this passionate tale of the Gaspesian village of L'Anse-aux-Corbeaux. The story follows Pauline, a strong and ambitious woman, and Noum, a stubborn scrapper, who have a moving love affair and try to improve their lives and those of their family by struggling against the exploitation of the fishers.

were little fishing villages. With a little imagination, you can almost hear the shouts of children playing on the grass, women talking as they lay fish out to dry, or men chatting at the general store. In the late 19th and early 20th century, Grande-Grave saw sustained economic activity from May to October. Hundreds of families living along the coast, as well as seasonal workers, caught the cod and processed it into a dried and salted final product, the famous Gaspé Cure, which they exported to Italy, Portugal, Spain, and the Antilles. The towns' entire existence centred around the companies that controlled the fisheries and thus the inhabitants' lives.

Grande-Grave is not a stage set or a reconstruction, but the very place where thousands of people lived, worked, loved, were born, and are buried. The costumed guides you will see and hear during your visit portray people who really lived here—humble folk who lived through misery and domination without losing their humanity and joie de vivre in this breathtaking natural setting.

Hyman & Sons, a Store at the Heart of the Village

The Hyman & Sons store had only been closed for three years when Forillon Park was created in 1970. Much more than just a general store, this business incarnated the power of the fishing companies over the people of Gaspésie, and a visit to the store helps visitors understand the international economic scope of the fishery. Beyond that, seeing last century's most popular products on the shelves, some reproduced and others authentic, is fun for the whole family.

The Blanchette Homestead

When you set foot the Blanchette house, you enter the daily life of a real family of L'Anse Blanchette. And not just any family; Monsieur Blanchette, a resourceful and easygoing man, was known as a skilful storyteller and excellent musician. His reincarnation instantly answers any questions and spins amazing tales to delight visitors. In the house, completely decorated with period furniture, costumed guides reveal the humble life of those who made their home here.

■ Natural Interpretation

A team of passionate naturalists offer numerous tours throughout the park to show visitors all of its most fascinating natural wonders. These informal activities, usually lasting about 1h30, bring together information, demonstration, and observation, fully involving the visitors. Ask the park staff or check the notice boards for dates, times, and places. While you're visiting the park, don't hesitate to ask the naturalists any questions you might have—that's what they're there for!

Hiking

Walking is by far the best way to explore and discover the park. Of the nine trails, several are suitable for the whole family, regardless of physical condition, while more challenging trails will delight intermediate or advanced hikers. Each leads to one or more points of interest, whether a remarkable ecosystem, a historic site, or a wonderful viewpoint. For example, the Mont Saint-Alban tower, 283m above sea level, offers a breathtaking view of the sea and mountains. The Les Graves trail follows the coastline where the Appalachians meet the sea. Elsewhere, just a few minutes' walk along the short La Chute trail leads to a beautiful natural wonder.

For long-distance hikers, the International Appalachian Trail (IAT) crosses the park for more than 50km west to east. The Québec section of the IAT ends (or starts) at Cap-Gaspé, at the far eastern tip of Forillon, and runs 650km to Mount Katahdin in the American state of Maine.

Information: ☎ 418-562-7885

■ Interpretive Trails

Prélude à Forillon

Length: 0.6km (loop)
Time: 30min
Level: easy

This short interpretive trail, accessible to physically disabled and visually impaired people, appeals to all the senses to present the theme of the park—harmony between man, land, and sea. A visit to the nearby Interpretation Centre completes this half-hour walk.

Une tournée dans les parages

Length: 3km (loop)
Time: 2h
Level: easy

History takes centre stage on this tour, which visits several points of interest. The trail starts near the fishing harbour, continues along Fruing Beach, passes the Hyman buildings to L'Anse-Blanchette, and takes you back through fields and woods to a number of old houses and barns. Outdoor exhibits along the way recount the history of Grande-Grave.

■ Hiking Trails

La Chute

Length: 1km (loop)
Time: 30min
Level: easy

This pleasant nature walk allows you to appreciate the beauty and diversity of the forest, spending just enough energy to admire the 17m waterfall at the end. The trail, with an altitude gain of about 50m, includes some wooden walkways as well as several stairs.

Les Graves

• **Departure from Grande-Grave**

Length: 15.2km (round trip)
Time: 4h30
Level: intermediate

• **Departure from L'Anse-aux-Amérindiens**

Length: 8km (round trip)
Time: 2h30
Level: easy

This seaside trail runs almost all the way along the south coast of the park as far as the tip of Presqu'île de Forillon. Pebble beaches, charming bays, and shorter cliffs than the north side are on display, and you may spot marine mammals offshore. You can also take a 3.2km gravel path as far as Cap-Gaspé.

Mont Saint-Alban

• **Departure from Petit-Gaspé beach**

Length: 7.2km (loop)
Time: 3h
Level: intermediate

• **Departure from Cap Bon Ami**

Length: 7.8km (loop)
Time: 3h
Level: intermediate
This trail passes Forillon's most spectacular natural landscapes, culminating an observation tower at 283m above sea level. Although the trail is somewhat steep at the beginning, the effort of the first few kilometres is more than repaid by the satisfaction of reaching the summit. The people of L'Anse-au-Griffon once travelled this trail with ox-drawn carts to buy supplies at Grande-Grave.

Les Crêtes

Length: 16.3km (one way) or 18.2km (one way) including access legs
Time: 6h30
Level: expert

This long trail runs through a wooded mountainous area. At different places, there are panoramic lookout points over the Anse-au-Griffon valley, the Gulf of St. Lawrence and Baie de Gaspé. It is possible to camp at two unserviced

camping areas located along the way. However, you are required to register at a reception centre or toll kiosks before setting out.

Les Lacs

Length: 16.8km (one way) or 17.6km (one way) including access legs
Time: 6h
Level: expert

The park's gateway to the International Appalachian Trail (IAT), this long-distance hike offers a majestic view of the Rivière au Renard valley. The route leads past a string of picturesque little lakes between two mountain crests. Hikers can use the wilderness camping area located along the trail.

Le Portage

Length: 10km (one-way)
Time: 3h
Level: intermediate

This trail is accessible to hikers, cyclists and horseback riders. Located in the southern part of the park, it goes through a wooded area, which opens up to the north onto fallow fields. This is a good place to observe bears, forest birds, and small mammals.

La Vallée

Length: 9.2km (round trip)
Time: 3h
Level: intermediate

This trail is for hikers, cyclists, and horseback riders who want to observe and listen to nature. It runs along the beautiful Rivière de l'Anse au Griffon and meets the Le Portage trail, following the forest edge where animals play early and late in the day.

Penouille

Length: 4km (round trip)
Time: 1h
Level: easy

This trail for hikers, cyclists, and in-line skaters links a wide variety of points of interest. Bring your field guides, binoculars, and camera. This walk might take longer than you think because something will tempt you to stop every ten metres! If you bring your bathing suit, you can enjoy the most beautiful beach in the area (changing rooms available). Picnic tables are available at the end. If you prefer, you can walk the whole length of the trail on the beach.

Information and Regulations:

Before setting out, always check the length of your hike. Bring water and, if desired, a snack. And above all, when hiking in Forillon, don't forget your binoculars and camera!

• For your safety, stick to the trails.

• Pack out all of your garbage, as there are no garbage cans on the trails.

Forillon National Park of Canada   –   Overview of Activities – Hiking

• Pets are allowed on the trails but must be kept on a leash at all times.

• Open fires are prohibited in the back country.

• Brochures on the trails and topographical maps are available at the Visitor Reception Centres and toll kiosks.

Cycling

Cycling is a good way to access certain parts of the park, allowing you to get a new perspective on nature and exercise at the same time. Bicycles are especially useful for getting around the campgrounds and getting to service centres or activities.

You can cycle the secondary roads in the North and South Areas, on the road on Penouille beach, and on Le Portage trail. Mountain bike riders can also take La Vallée trail and the gravel path to Cap Gaspé. However, bicycles are prohibited on the other hiking trails. Bicycles can be rented at the park recreation centre and at the L'Anse-aux-Amérindiens parking lot. The latter is a good starting point for an easy ride up the coast to Cap Gaspé, but only real afi-cionados ride up the last slope to the lighthouse; most will leave their bikes at the foot of the slope and walk up.

In-Line Skating

In-line skaters can use the park and campground access roads, which are paved and, especially in the south, not especially steep. However, the best place to in-line skate is at the Penouille beach, with 2km of asphalt trail. Short stretches at the beginning may be damaged by storms, but the rest is usually in perfect condition as it is slightly farther from the shore. It is possible to skate from the parking lot to the trailhead nearby.

Horseback Riding

Riders can explore the park by taking the Le Portage and La Vallée trails as well as certain parts of the park's southern boundary corridor. Guided riding excursions are available near the park. Ask a park attendant for information.

Picnicking

Enjoy the calm and beauty of nature in the park's picnic areas. L'Anse-aux-Amérindiens, L'Anse-Saint-Georges, and Fort-Péninsule have designated picnic areas. Other sites, such as Grande-Grave and Cap Bon Ami, are equipped with picnic shelters. In Penouille, visitors can enjoy picnic tables, a beach, a recreation ground and a service building with toilets and showers. You can walk to the site or access it for a small fee by public transportation.

Activities at the Recreation Centre

Located in the South Area of the park, the Recreation Centre provides many activities and services for the entire family. Visitors can enjoy a refreshing dip in the heated outdoor swimming pool or splash in the wading pool. They can also play tennis, volleyball, or shuffleboard, or use the playground. A bike rental service is available on site. Please note that there are fees for the use of the swimming pool and tennis courts.

The swimming pool is open daily from 9:30am to 12:30pm and 1pm to 5pm from mid-June to the third week of August.

Nautical Activities

■ Cruises

Panorama-Découverte Excursion

Several times a day, an interpretation cruise lets visitors discover the spectacular beauty of the park's north shore, with its dizzying cliffs, sea mammals, and bird colonies. The cruise starts from the Des-Rosiers campground and passes by Cap Bon Ami to the end of the peninsula.

Early June to mid-September.

Departure from the North Area Interpretation Centre.

■ Sea Kayaking

Numerous excursions are available, including two 2h outings. One takes you to a seal colony where you can watch or take magnificent photos of the animals basking on the rocks or playing in the water around you. The other leads along the south coast of the park,

Safety Regulations for Sea Activities at Forillon National Park

Forillon National Park's seaside location attracts an increasing number of visitors interested in pleasure boating, sea kayaking, scuba diving and other ocean activities. To ensure your safety and the protection of resources, please follow the safety regulations that apply to water sports.

Let someone know what you are planning to do; whenever possible, use the buddy system. Always inform someone of your departure and arrival points as well as the time you expect to return.

Check the weather and the tides—weather conditions can change quickly at sea, and wind and fog can arrive suddenly. Tides can cause strong currents that may be difficult to overcome.

Bring along the safety equipment you need and learn how to use it in case of an emergency. Above all, never go beyond your limits.

with the eroded cliffs and historic buildings as a backdrop. Early birds and night owls can enjoy the beautiful spectacle of the sunrise or sunset over Baie de Gaspé. There are also night excursions with amazing sights such as bioluminescence, northern lights, and shooting stars. When weather permits, you can also take part in a one-day excursion around the peninsula or to Penouille beach. Whatever you choose, you can be sure of quality service from the guides, who have been certified by Québec's canoeing and kayaking federation. All equipment is provided. Guided tours are available from early June to mid-September.

■ Snorkelling and Scuba Diving

The sea floor around Forillon delights divers with its abundant, colourful and supremely diverse marine life. Every one of the stone blocks that erosion has scoured from the cliffs of Forillon and thrown to the seabed is a haven for sea life, both plants and animals. Add to that an exceptionally active, nutrient-rich environment produced by the meeting of the waters of the St. Lawrence and Baie de Gaspé, and you have all the elements for a truly fascinating dive. The best diving takes place at three sites: Petit-Gaspé, Grande-Grave, and L'Anse-Saint-Georges. In Grande-Grave, divers can use a service building with lockers and basins for rinsing out their equipment.

In all, a dozen diving sites are distributed along the south shore of the peninsula and point. The cold oxygenated waters host numerous anemones, soft corals, lobsters, and forests of sea cabbage. Sometimes, friendly seals come by to say hello.

■ Swimming

The sandy beach of Pointe de Penouille is a great spot for swimming, and the shallow waters warm up fairly well in the summer. An inexpensive shuttle is available to take you from the Reception Centre to the beach 2km away. Bathers have a playground and service building with toilets and showers at their disposal.

The Recreation Centre in the South Area welcomes people of all ages in its heated swimming pool and wading pool.

■ Fishing

Mackerel and plaice are among the fish that anglers can catch from the Grande-Grave dock (South Area). More than a hobby, fishing also offers the chance to meet and chat with local residents who come to the docks to try their luck during the summer. Some regulations apply to ensure anglers' safety and protect the resource:

• The daily limit for mackerel is 10 catches per angler, including mackerel that are caught and released.

• No person may have more than 10 mackerel in his or her possession at any time.

• Anglers may not use more than a single line with one single or triple hook.

• Permits are not required.

■ Beach Activities

It's a treat to walk along a pebble beach, soothed by the rhythm of waves and swell. The beaches at Cap-Bon-Ami, Petit-Gaspé, Grande-Grave, and the Des-Rosiers campground are sure to please. You can also swim and wade at Penouille's splendid sandy beach (take note that there is no lifeguard service at this beach). The beach offers picnic areas, playgrounds, and a service building with washrooms and showers.

■ Yachting

Pleasure craft can dock at two marinas near Forillon Park: at Rivière-au-Renard to the north and Gaspé to the south.

Winter Activities

■ Winter Camping

Like many national parks, Forillon allows and encourages winter camping. Winter campers are welcome at the Petit-Gaspé group campground in the South Area. This campground, about 2km from the parking lot, is accessible by snowshoes or skis on an ungroomed trail.

Registration is required and camping fees are payable at the park's administration office or operational centre.

■ Cross-Country Skiing

Skiers can enjoy their favourite sport on more than 40km of maintained trails. For their added comfort, there are shelters equipped with wood stoves, picnic tables and dry toilets along most trails.

There are three departure points for the cross-country ski trails:

• Le Portage parking area near Penouille;

• La Vallée parking area at L'Anse-au-Griffon;

• Le Castor parking area near Cap-des-Rosiers.

La Vallée

Length: 9.2km (round trip)
Access: 1km from Route 132 at L'Anse-au-Griffon

On fairly flat terrain, sheltered from the wind, this trail follows Rivière de l'Anse au Griffon and eventually reaches Le Portage trail. A shelter is located at the trail's mid-point.

La Cédrière

Length: 11km (loop)
Access: Via La Vallée or Le Ruisseau trails

This trail takes skiers to the park's mountainous heights. Along the way, you will come across a two-hundred-year-old cedar grove.

Le Ruisseau

Length: 9.6km (loop)
Access: Via La Cédrière trail to the west or Le Castor trail from the east

The Le Ruisseau trail takes you over hill and dale through the scenic countryside.

Le Castor

Length: 7.6km (loop)
Access: Via Route 132, 5km from Cap-des-Rosiers, or via Le Ruisseau trail to the west

This trail crosses the Cap-des-Rosiers lowlands. You will discover a magnificent maple grove.

Le Portage

Length: 20km (round trip)
Access: 0.5km from Route 132 near Penouille, or 1km from Route 132 at L'Anse-au-Griffon

In the south, the trail passes through a wooded area, and opens onto fields further north. It joins La Vallée and La Cédrière trails.

Regulations

- A daily or annual permit is required for all skiers using the groomed trails in the park. Permits are available at the park's administration office, at the operational centre, and at certain retailers located near the trails.

- Marked and maintained trails are for skiers exclusively.

- Domestic animals are not allowed in shelters and on trails, except on Le Portage trail where dogsledding is permitted.

- It is forbidden to sleep in kitchen shelters.

- In case of difficulty: ☎418-892-5553 or 418-368-6440 (outside of office hours).

■ Snowshoes

Many areas in the park are well suited for snowshoeing.

■ Dogsledding

This increasingly popular activity can be practiced on Le Portage trail.

Practical Information

Universal Access

■ Reception

The reception centres of L'Anse-au-Griffon and Penouille have parking spaces, washrooms, water fountains and counters accessible to persons with disabilities. Reception staff have also received special training to better respond to the needs of this clientele.

■ Exhibitions

To respond to the needs of park users with reduced mobility, some parts of the park, including Grande-Grave and L'Anse-Blanchette, offer alternative programs. Photo albums have been created to demonstrate exhibits that are difficult or impossible to reach for the mobility impaired. At Fort-Péninsule, interpretation and orientation panels have been created and strategically placed to make it easier to move around the fort.

For people with auditory disabilities, the films *Time and Tide Remembered* (15min), *The Underwater Life of the Gulf of St. Lawrence* (54min) and *Homarus Americanus* (27min) are subtitled in both English and French.

■ Trail

The interpretive trail Prélude à Forillon has been adapted for users with physical and visual disabilities.

Lodging

Forillon Park offers 367 semi-serviced campsites as well as a group campground. There are three campgrounds—Des-Rosiers and Cap-Bon-Ami, in the North Area, and Petit-Gaspé, in the South Area.

About a quarter of these campsites are available each day for campers without reservations. Most are in wooded areas, and provide good privacy. Only the Cap-Bon-Ami campsite offers an open environment, exposed to the wind but with a panoramic view of the Gulf of St. Lawrence as well as beach access. This unserviced campground is reserved for primitive camping and small RVs. Certain campsites in the Des-Rosiers campground overlook the river, and are all are just a short walk from the beach.

The serviced campgrounds have individual power plugs and water outlets nearby. Dumping stations, garbage cans, and recycling bins are found at the exit of the campgrounds.

Three wilderness camping locations are located in the backcountry along the Les Crêtes and Les Lacs trails.

Since the winter of 2007, the park has offered five yurts and several unserviced shelters for rent through a concessionaire, **Les Petites Maisons du Parc** *(☎418-892-5873 or 1-866-892-5873, www.gesmat.ca)*. Yurts can sleep four and have a stove, a refrigerator, and a complete set of dishes. Unserviced shelters sleep six to eight. Pit toilets are located near the yurts and shelters, and the concessionaire brings drinking water each day.

■ Fees

Entry and service fees are charged at most national parks and national historic sites, where revenues go to support visitor services and facilities. This means that every time you visit a park or site you are investing in its future—and in a legacy for future generations.

The following definitions apply to entry and service fee categories unless otherwise specified:

Adult: person 17 to 64 years of age
Senior: person 65 years of age or over
Youth: person 6 to 16 years of age
Family/group: up to seven people with a maximum of two adults arriving at a national park in a single vehicle or visiting a national historic site together
School groups: elementary and secondary school students

We suggest checking for fee schedule updates each year after April 1:

www.pc.gc.ca/forillon

■ Reservation Service

To ensure that you will have a campsite for your visit to Forillon, it is recommended to use the Parks Canada Campground Reservation Service:

☎877-737-3783 or 1-866-787-6221 (TTY for hearing-impaired callers)
www.pccamping.ca

For a reservation at the Petit-Gaspé group campground, con-

Forillon National Park of Canada - Practical Information - Lodging

tact the park office at ☎418-368-5505 or 418-892-5911.

Out of the park's 367 campsites, about a quarter remain available for campers without prior reservations. Unreserved campsites are assigned on a first-come, first-served basis.

■ Primitive Camping on the Trails

Backcountry campsites are located along Les Crêtes and Les Lacs trails. These sites include basic amenities, such as pit toilets and picnic tables. There is no cost for camping at backcountry sites, but registration at a reception centre or toll kiosk is mandatory. Open-air wood fires are prohibited in all areas of the backcountry.

■ Information and Regulations

To protect resources and ensure the safety and well-being of visitors, parks are governed by a number of regulations, notably the following.

You are not allowed to:

• hunt, trap, disturb, attract or feed the animals;

• fish in fresh water (ponds, lakes, rivers, creeks, etc.);

• remove, mutilate or destroy any natural features (wildlife, plants, fossils, driftwood, deadwood, etc.);

• make wood fires anywhere except in fireplaces provided for this purpose;

• camp outside designated campsites;

• make excessive noise at any time;

• let pets wander freely (without a leash);

• operate a personal watercraft (Seadoo™, etc.) in park waters.

Remember that seatbelts must be worn when riding in vehicles and that the Highway Safety Code applies at all times.

For more information, contact a park warden at ☎418-892-5553.

■ Lodging Outside the Park

There are also private campgrounds (with and without services) near the park. For visitors who prefer other types of lodging, the towns and villages neighbouring the park can

Campgrounds in the Park

Petit-Gaspé (South Area) until mid-September

Without electricity: 136 sites	• Wooded campground • Recreation Centre (with restaurant, swimming pool and laundromat nearby)
With electricity: 35 sites	• Talks at the amphitheatre • Dumping station at the campground entrance • Water outlets along the loops

Des-Rosiers (North Area) until mid-October

Without electricity: 113 sites	• Semi-wooded campground • Talks at the amphitheatre
With electricity: 42 sites	• Dumping station at the campground entrance • Water outlets along the loops

Cap-Bon-Ami (North Area) until early September

Without electricity: 41 sites	• Unwooded campground • Lookout and trail nearby

Petit-Gaspé group campsite (South Area) year-round

Without electricity: 4 areas	• Groups of 10 people or more, maximum 100 campers Reservations required: ☎418-368-5505 ☎418-892-5911 (summer)

accommodate them. There are motels, hotels, inns, cottages, cabins, and several bed and breakfasts close by.

For more information on lodging, restaurants, and other services near the park, contact Office du Tourisme et des Congrès de Gaspé, which deals with a large part of the tip of the Gaspé Peninsula in addition to the city of Gaspé itself.

Office du Tourisme et des Congrès de Gaspé
27 Boulevard York Est
Gaspé, Québec G4X 2K9
☎ 418-368-8525
🖶 418-368-8549
www.tourismegaspe.org

Dining

Visitors of Forillon National Park can grab a bite at the Recreation Centre restaurant, located in the South Area of the Park. The restaurant is open from early June to early September. Besides that, a very diversified catering trade is offered in the surroundings of Forillon. From friendly snack bars to the finest regional gastronomy, restaurateurs from the areas are sure to satisfy everyone's appetite.

To feed your sweet tooth or relax for a while in a comfortable atmosphere, Café du Manoir, at the Centre socioculturel du Manoir Le Boutillier in L'Anse-au-Griffon, serves good coffee with pastries, as well as afternoon tea.

Campers always end up running low on milk or butter or something else. Happily, two grocery stores are located near the park entrances. To stock up on fish and seafood before setting up camp, stop at the markets of Rivière-au-Renard, Québec's fishing capital.

Nearby

Rivière-au-Renard

Centre d'interprétation des pêches
☎ 418-269-3788 or 418-269-7358
Québec's fishing capital, Rivière-au-Renard has always had major fishing industry facilities that in recent years have evolved impressively. In the middle of this busy environment, a lively, concrete interpretive visit is offered amidst the fishers and processing plants. This is your chance to discover the world of the St. Lawrence fishery.

L'Anse-au-Griffon

Centre socioculturel du manoir Le Boutillier
mid-June to early October
every day 9am to 5pm
entrance fee
578 Boulevard Griffon
☎418-892-5150
www.lansequgriffon.ca

Originally from Jersey in the Channel Islands, John Le Boutillier was one of the most important cod merchants of his day. His magnificent mansion, built around 1850, is now a historic monument and a national historic site of Canada. Half-hour guided tours transport you to the mid-19th century, when the building served as the headquarters for John Le Boutillier and Co. You can also stroll around the grounds on a footpath. Le Café du Manoir serves coffee and pastries as well as afternoon tea at 5pm. Stop in to visit the La Morue Verte souvenir shop and exhibit.

Centre culturel Le Griffon
557 Boulevard Griffon
☎418-892-0115
www.lanseaugriffon.ca

Set up in an old cold-storage warehouse built in 1942, this unique cultural centre houses an exhibition hall and an artist's workshop, as well as Internet access and Café de l'Anse. Shows and summer theatre from Thursday to Saturday. Dinner-theatre packages (reservations: ☎418-360-3688).

Cap-des-Rosiers

Cap-des-Rosiers Lighthouse National Historic Site of Canada
884 Boulevard Anse-à-la-Renommée
☎418-269-3310
www.pc.gc.ca

The Cap-des-Rosiers lighthouse is without a doubt the most photographed historic attraction on the peninsula. Seen from the east of Cap des Rosiers, the sunset over the lighthouse is remarkable. The site, dotted with the rosebushes that gave it its name, is irresistibly charming. It was from this cape in 1759, that an officer spotted the fleet of General Wolfe coming up the St. Lawrence to take Québec City. The courier that the soldier sent proved of little help to the French.

After numerous shipwrecks, including the *Carrick's*, long engraved in the collective memory of the Gaspé, the Cap-des-Rosiers lighthouse was built in 1858. Classed as a national historic site in 1977, at 37m it is still the tallest lighthouse in Canada.

Forillon National Park of Canada - Practical Information - Nearby

Forillon

Fort-Péninsule
Boulevard Forillon

Built during the Second World War, this naval defence system is now within Forillon Park limits. A visit reveals a forgotten part of history thanks to the interpretive tour.

Fontenelle

Gespeg Mi'kmaq interpretation site
783 Boulevard Pointe-Navarre
☎ 418-368-7449
www.gaspesie.com/gespeg

The Mi'kmaq nation, which has lived in the Gaspé region for centuries, invites you to discover how they lived in the 17th century through a guided tour of the traditional village. A multipurpose building houses an exhibit of crafts, a gift shop, and workshops.

Gaspé

Musée de la Gaspésie
80 Boulevard de Gaspé
☎ 418-368-1534
www.museedelagaspesie.ca

In addition to exhibits on the history and culture of Gaspésie, Musée de la Gaspésie presents *Jacques Cartier, la découverte d'un Nouveau Monde*, the largest exhibit ever created on the French explorer's first voyage in 1534.

Jacques Cartier Monument National Historic Site of Canada

Located near Musée de la Gaspésie on Pointe Jacques-Cartier, this national historic site commemorates the memorable encounter of European and Aboriginal cultures in 1534, when Jacques Cartier arrived in Canada.

APPENDIX

Index

Notes

Notes

Our Guides

Fabulous
Fabulous Western Canada	CAD$ 29.95	USD$ 32.95
Fabulous Montréal	CAD$ 29.95	USD$ 27.95
Fabulous Québec	CAD$ 29.95	USD$ 22.95

Ulysses - Special Collection
Illustrated Canada Map for Kids	CAD$ 22.95	USD$ 22.95

Ulysses Green Escapes
Cross-Country Skiing and Snowshoeing in Ontario	CAD$ 24.95	USD$ 22.95
Cycling in France	CAD$ 22.95	USD$ 17.95
Cycling in Ontario	CAD$ 24.95	USD$ 17.95
Hiking in Ontario	CAD$ 24.95	USD$ 19.95
Hiking in Québec	CAD$ 24.95	USD$ 19.95
National Parks in Gaspésie and Bas-Saint-Laurent		
Ontario's Bike Paths and Rail Trails	CAD$ 22.95	USD$ 17.95
The Trans Canada Trail in Québec	CAD$ 24.95	USD$ 19.95

Ulysses in Mind
Montréal in Mind	CAD$ 12.95	USD$ 13.95

Ulysses Phrasebooks
Canadian French for Better Travel	CAD$ 9.95	USD$ 6.95
French for Better Travel	CAD$ 9.95	USD$ 6.95
Italian for Better Travel	CAD$ 9.95	USD$ 7.95
Spanish for Better Travel in Latin America	CAD$ 9.95	USD$ 7.95
Spanish for Better Travel in Spain	CAD$ 9.95	USD$ 7.95
Universal Communicator	CAD$ 9.95	USD$ 11.95

Ulysses Travel Guides
Atlantic Canada	CAD$ 24.95	USD$ 19.95
Canada	CAD$ 29.95	USD$ 22.95
Montréal	CAD$ 24.95	USD$ 22.95
Ontario	CAD$ 32.95	USD$ 28.95
Panamá	CAD$ 27.95	USD$ 19.95
Québec	CAD$ 29.95	USD$ 27.95
Québec City	CAD$ 24.95	USD$ 24.95
Toronto	CAD$ 22.95	USD$ 17.95
Vancouver, Victoria and Whistler	CAD$ 19.95	USD$ 14.95
Western Canada	CAD$ 29.95	USD$ 22.95

Ulysses Travel Journals
Travel Journal: The Lighthouse	CAD$ 12.95	USD$ 9.95

Titles	Quantity	Price	Total

Name:	Subtotal	
	Shipping	CAD$ 4.99/USD $7.50
Address:	GST (in Canada)	
	Total	
E-mail:		

Payment: ☐ Cheque ☐ Visa ☐ MasterCard

Card number _____ Expiry date _____

Signature _____

To place an order, please send this order form to one of our offices (the adresses appear on the following page), or visit our Web site: **www.ulyssesguides.com**.

Contact Information

Offices
Canada: Ulysses Travel Guides, 4176 Saint-Denis Street, Montréal, Québec, H2W 2M5, ☎514-843-9447, ▤514-843-9448, info@ulysses.ca, www.ulyssesguides.com

Europe: Les Guides de Voyage Ulysse SARL, 127 rue Amelot, 75011 Paris, France, ☎01 43 38 89 50, voyage@ulysse.ca, www.ulyssesguides.com

Distributors
U.S.A.: Hunter Publishing, 130 Campus Drive, Edison, NJ 08818, ☎800-255-0343, ▤732-417-1744 or 0482, comments@hunterpublishing.com, www.hunterpublishing.com

Canada: Ulysses Travel Guides, 4176 Saint-Denis Street, Montréal, Québec, H2W 2M5, ☎514-843-9882, ext. 2232, ▤514-843-9448, info@ulysses.ca, www.ulyssesguides.com

Great Britain and Ireland: Roundhouse Publishing, Millstone, Limers Lane, Northam, North Devon, EX39 2RG, ☎1 202 66 54 32, ▤1 202 66 62 19, roundhouse.group@ukgateway.net

Other countries: Ulysses Travel Guides, 4176 Saint-Denis Street, Montréal, Québec, H2W 2M5, ☎514-843-9882, ext.2232, ▤514-843-9448, info@ulysses.ca, www.ulyssesguides.com

Write to Us

The information contained in this guide was correct at press time. However, mistakes may slip by, omissions are always possible, establishments may move, etc. The authors and publisher hereby disclaim any liability for loss or damage resulting from omissions or errors.

We value your comments, corrections and suggestions, as they allow us to keep each guide up to date. The best contributions will be rewarded with a free book from Ulysses Travel Guides. All you have to do is write us at the following address and indicate which title you would be interested in receiving (please refer to the list provided in the previous pages).

Ulysses Travel Guides
4176 Saint-Denis Street
Montréal (Québec)
Canada H2W 2M5
www.ulyssesguides.com
E-mail: text@ulysses.ca

Contact Information - Write to Us

Parc national du Bic

Location

Forestville

Longue-Rive

Les Escoumins

Saint Lawrence River

Île du Bic

Parc national du Bic

Rimouski
Le Bic
Saint-Fabien
Saint-Simon
Trois-Pistoles

Île aux Basques
Île-Verte

L'Isle-Verte

0 5 10 20 30 40 Km

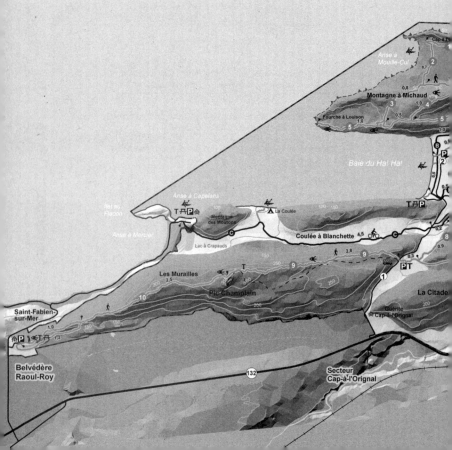

Cap

Anse à
Mouillé-Cul

2

0,7

0,8

Montagne à Michaud

4

Fourche à Louison
1,0

0,5

5

5

B

P
2

Baie du Ha! Ha!

T P

0,9

Anse à Capelans

100

La Coulée

100 150

8

Montagne
des Moutons

Anse à Mercier

C

Coulée à Blanchette 4,5

C

0,2

0,9

Ilet au
Flacon

Lac à Crapauds

2,8

9

0,3

150

250

9

PT

Les Murailles
2,5

T

250

1

La Citadel

Pic Champlain

200

250

Guérite
Cap-à-l'Orignal

Saint-Fabien-
sur-Mer

10

200

1,0

P

132

Belvédère
Raoul-Roy

Secteur
Cap-à-l'Orignal

Legend

Zones

- Ambient and Service Zones
- Conservation Zone
- Extreme Conservation Zone
- Park Limits

Trails and Roads

- Bicycle Trails
- Hiking Trails
- Not Serviced
- Difficult at High-Tide
- Railroad Track
- Main Road
- Secondary Road
- Shuttle

- Information Kiosk
- Collection Booth
- Discovery and Service Centre
- Historical Building
- Launching Ramp
- Docking Basin
- Departure Point for Sea Kayak and Zodiac Trips
- Picnic Area

- Camping
- Convenience Store
- Croque-Nature (Food Stand)
- Vending Machine
- Nature Store
- Amphitheater
- Autorized Stopping
- Look-out

- Observation Area
- Comfort Station
- Pit toilet
- Parking
- Shuttle
- Facilities For The Disabled
- Seal-Watching
- Yurt

Saint Lawrence River

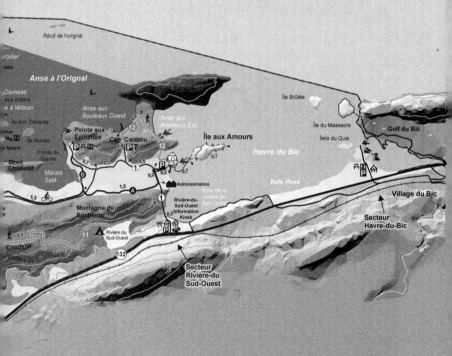

Récif de l'orignal

Anse à l'Orignal

Cap Enragé

Île Brûlée

Île du Massacre

Golf du Bic

Anse aux Bouleaux Ouest

Anse aux Bouleaux Est

Île aux Amours

Îlets du Quai

Havre du Bic

Pointe aux Épinettes

Cap Caribou

Baie Rose

Village du Bic

Administration

Anse de la rivière du Sud-Ouest

Rivière-du-Sud-Ouest Information Kiosk

Secteur Havre-du-Bic

Montagne du Bûcheron

Rivière du Sud-Ouest

Secteur Rivière-du-Sud-Ouest

Citadelle

Rivière du Sud-Ouest

132

Mont Chocolat

Marais Salé

Pointe du Glacier

Île Ronde

Île aux Canards

aux Eiders

e à Wilson

Damase

Voilier

Scale   1:32 000

0   250 500   1 000   1 500   2 000   2 500
Metres

Parc national de la Gaspésie

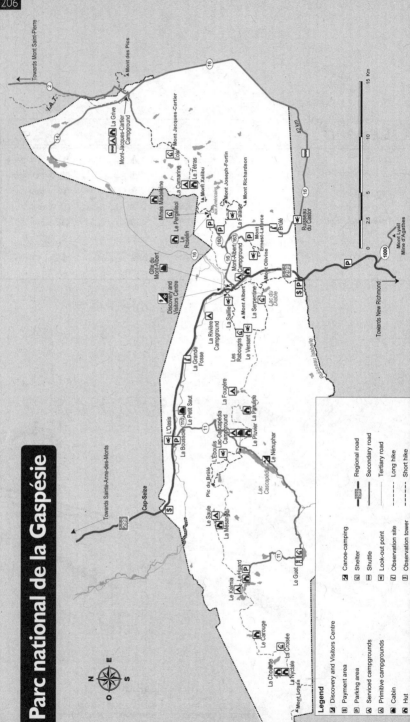

Legend

- **Discovery and Visitors Centre**
- **$** Payment area
- **P** Parking area
- **Serviced campgrounds**
- **Primitive campgrounds**
- **Cabin**
- **Hut**
- **Canoe-camping**
- **Shelter**
- **Shuttle**
- **Look-out point**
- **Observation site**
- **Observation tower**

	Regional road
	Secondary road
	Tertiary road
	Long hike
	Short hike

0   2.5   5   10   15 Km

Parc national de l'Île-Bonaventure-et-du-Rocher-Percé

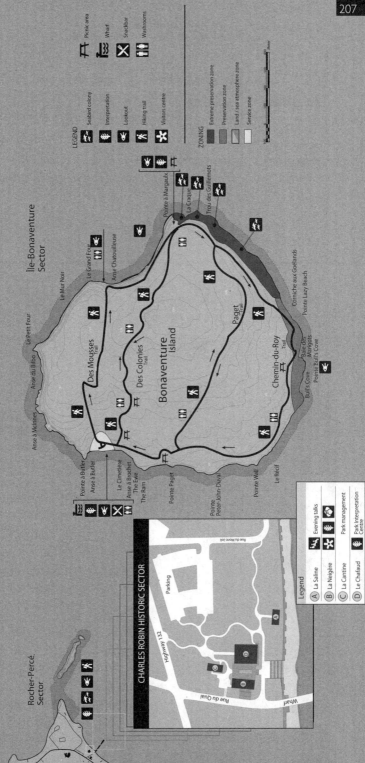

Rocher-Percé Sector

Île-Bonaventure Sector

LEGEND

- Seabird colony
- Interpretation
- Lookout
- Hiking Trail
- Visitors centre

- Picnic area
- Wharf
- Snackbar
- Washrooms

ZONING

- Extreme preservation zone
- Preservation zone
- Land / sea atmosphere zone
- Service zone

Bonaventure Island

Des Mousses Trail
Des Colonies Trail
Paget Trail
Chemin-du-Roy Trail

Le Grand Four
Anse Chatouilleuse
Le Mur Noir
Le Petit Four
Anse du Bilbo
Anse à McInnes
Pointe à Butler
Anse à Butler
Le Cimetière
Anse à Brochet
The Ewe
The Ram
Pointe Paget
Pointe Peter-John-Duval
Pointe Wall
Le Récif
Bull's Cove
Pointe Bull's Cove
Baie des Margots
Pointe Lazy Beach
Corniche aux Goélands

Pointe à Margaulx
La Coque
Trou des Guillemots

CHARLES ROBIN HISTORIC SECTOR

Highway 132
Rue du Quai
Wharf
Parking
Rue du Mont-Joli

Legend

- Ⓐ La Saline
- Ⓑ La Neigère
- Ⓒ La Cantine
- Ⓓ Le Chafaud

- Evening talks
- Park management
- Park Interpretation Centre

Forillon National Park of Canada

SERVICES

- Campground
- Group campground
- Wilderness campsite
- Public transit
- St. Peter's Church
- Accessible to physically impaired

ACTIVITIES

- Playground area
- Swimming
- Cruise
- Horseback riding
- Fishing
- Picnicking
- Scuba diving
- Hiking
- Backpacking
- Mountain biking
- Cycling
- Sea kayaking
- Recreation Centre

FACILITIES

- Interpretation Centre
- Amphitheatre
- Lookout
- Heritage site
- Interpretation panel
- Visitor reception centre
- Toll booth
- Shelter
- Artillery gun
- Lighthouse
- Observation tower
- Hiking trail
- Bicycle trail
- Distance (km) between 2 points
- Park's boundary
- Main road
- Paved secondary road

Prohibited or restricted access zones – at certain times of the year, activities such as scuba diving, hiking or mooring are not allowed in this area. Ask a Park employee for information.

DISTANCES (KM)

	Gaspé
Penouille	20
Grande-Grave	18	38
South Area	5	13	33
North Area	10	15	23	43
L'Anse-au-Griffon	18	28	33	41	61

GULF OF ST. LAWRENCE

CAP-DES-ROSIERS

L'ANSE-AU-GRIFFON

RIVIÈRE-AU-RENARD

VISITOR RECEPTION CENTRE

INTERNATIONAL APPALACHIAN TRAIL (IAT)

Lac-au-Renard

«Les Lacs» 4.5

«Le Portage» 2.2

Lac-de-Penouille

«La Vallée» 5.2

«Les Crêtes» 4.5

«La Chute» 3

«Le Castor»

1.4

4.7

4.8

4.5

OPERATIONAL CENTRE

FORT PENINSULE

VISITOR RECEPTION CENTRE

PENOUILLE

JACQUES CARTIER MONUMENT

GASPÉ

SAINT-MAJORIQUE

Sainte-Anne-des-Monts

NORTH AREA

INTERPRETATION CENTRE

«Prélude à Forillons»

DES-ROSIERS

CAP-BON-AMI

«Mont Saint-Alban» 4.3

IAT

«Une tournée dans les parages» 3 km

«Les Graves» IAT

CAP-GASPÉ

ANSE-AUX-AMÉRINDIENS (Anse-aux-Sauvages)

ANSE-SAINT-GEORGES

GRANDE-GRAVE

ANSE-BLANCHETTE

Petit-Gaspé Beach

SOUTH AREA

PETIT-GASPÉ

CAP-AUX-OS

GASPÉ BAY

GASPÉ

Percé

0 1 km